TAKE
BACK
YOUR
POWER

TAKE BACK YOUR POWER

How to Reclaim It, Keep It, and Use It to Get What You Deserve

 Yasmin Davidds

ATRIA BOOKS

NEW YORK LONDON TORONTO SYDNEY

ATRIA BOOKS

1230 Avenue of the Americas
New York, NY 10020

Library of Congress Cataloging in Publication Data
Davidds-Garrido, Yasmin.
Take back your power : how to reclaim it, keep it, and use it to get what you deserve /
Yasmin Davidds.—1st Atria Books trade pbk. ed.
p.   cm.
1. Hispanic American women—Life skills guides. 2. Hispanic American women—Social
conditions. 3. Hispanic American women—Psychology. 4. Conduct of life. 5. Control
(Psychology) 6. Power (Philosophy) 7. Sex role—United States. 8. Sex (Psychology) 9.
Man-woman relationship—United States. 10. Family—United States. I. Title.
E184.S75D355   2006
305.48'868073—dc22   2006045868
ISBN-13: 978-0-7432-8508-7
ISBN-10:   0-7432-8508-5

First Atria Books trade paperback edition June 2006

10 9 8 7 6 5 4 3 2 1

ATRIA BOOKS is a trademark of Simon & Schuster, Inc.

Manufactured in the United States of America

For information regarding special discounts for bulk purchases,
please contact Simon & Schuster Special Sales at
1-800-456-6798 or business@simonandschuster.com.

Grateful thanks to the following:

Steven Carter and Julia Sokol for granting us permission to use excerpts from their book
Men Love Women Who Love Themselves (New York: Dell Publishing, 1996).
    Claudia Colindres and Third Woman Press for permission to print an excerpt from
the book *The Sexuality of Latinas* (Berkeley: Third Woman Press, 1989).

To the Powerful Women in My Family
   My loving Mami, for your unconditional love . . . my
   beautiful sister, Judy, for your constant source of
   strength and support . . . my soul sister, Karina, for
   your protection up above the clouds . . . my beloved
   daughter, Divina, for your love that is so pure and
   precious . . . and my adoring niece, Isabella, whose
   presence in this world has brought new meaning to
   life

To My Sisters in Spirit
   Yvonne Lucas, Alexandria Olmos, Carrie Lopez,
   Nancy Landa, Ruth Livier, Sylvia Martinez, Michelle
   Dulong, and Xitlalt Herrera, whose constant source
   of love has given me unlimited strength and undeni-
   able courage

and

To the One Man Who Has to Put Up with Us All
   My brother-in-law, Michael Wright, for your devotion and protection

I love you with all my heart!

Empowerment

1. The act of investing oneself with power
2. The process of enabling or permitting oneself the right to succeed
3. The ability to be in control of one's own destiny
4. The strength to make the most of one's potential
5. The determination to define life by one's own terms

Contents

CONTENTS

TAKE
BACK
YOUR
POWER

WHY THIS BOOK

Who needs another female self-empowerment book? Consider the following:

- If in your need for approval and what you consider to be "love" you allow disrespect in your life, you are giving your power away.
- If you are not "standing in your truth," you are giving your power away.
- If you allow someone to speak to you in a derogatory or degrading way, you are giving your power away.
- If you don't speak up when you know you should, you are giving your power away.
- If you lower your standards in order to be accepted or liked, you are giving your power away.
- If you are not your authentic self, you are giving your power away.
- If you stay in situations you know are not good for you, you are giving your power away.
- If you say yes when you want to say no, you are giving your power away.
- If you agree with people you know are wrong, you are giving your power away.
- If you stay silent when you know you should speak up, you are giving your power away.
- If whatever you are made to feel ashamed of is what you really are, you are giving your power away.

- If you allow negative influences to invade your mind and sap your energy, you are giving your power away.
- If you do something you don't really believe in, you are giving your power away.
- If you live life on life's terms instead of your own terms, you are giving your power away.

If any of the above rings a bell deep inside your head, this book is for you.

I dedicate this book to every woman who has ever felt sad, frustrated, alone, scared, unsatisfied, compromised, or depleted. I know how it feels—I've been there, too. But I also know how it feels to be completely satisfied, self-aware, respected, confident, and powerful because I learned some very profound truths along the way. Think about it. Who are you really living your life for? What forces are influencing your decisions? How did you come to be the woman you are today? If your answers don't lead straight back to you, if you are living someone else's version of your life, the truths I share in this book are invaluable to you.

This book is about your inherent power—that internal flame you've either fed or stifled for most of your life. Your power is your life force, and you must learn about it and honor it if you want to be a whole woman. Do you remember the essence that sparked your dreams and imagination when you were a child? The natural instinct you took for granted that quelled your fears and gave you the confidence to express the real you? By rediscovering that spark, and then maintaining the fire that grows from it, you can reclaim your power and live life on your terms. There is no reason your desires and goals should ever be beyond your grasp, because, ultimately, *you* hold the key to your future. You can choose either to fuel your fire or to allow others to diminish the flame to a flicker, perpetuating everything that's holding you back.

If you want to control your own life, you must learn to make your own decisions. If you want the ability to bring *your* purpose to the world, your first commitment must be to reclaim and protect your life force, which is your power. Women who own their power are beautiful losers in the sense that they have lost all fear of shame, embarrassment, and criticism. They have lost all unnecessary inhibitions and concern for what other people "might think," and they take risks they have weighed carefully because they have no choice but to honor their inner voice.

It's every woman's dream to find success and happiness. I am here to tell you that all things are possible—even if you are on the verge of giving up. Women who have made successful changes in their lives have had to fight. I know from experience. And by studying the lives, mindsets, and habits of empowered women, I learned just how similar we all are. Every woman has a unique story, though we've often been taught to keep our thoughts and opinions private. If you can break free from negative cultural messages and see yourself in a new light, you can be unstoppable. When you analyze your past and the influences that affected your development, you can learn to break patterns that are holding you back from realizing your true potential. There is a diamond in the rough that lies deep in your soul—teach it to sparkle like the precious gem it is. Once you recognize the impact your subconscious mind has, you can use your own power—in the form of intuition, faith, courage, and self-respect—to become the writer and director of your own life story. When we are given the opportunity to learn about ourselves, we turn the power on, we realize our dreams, and we pass our successes to future generations.

To all women whose hearts are aching for courage and inspiration:

We need to begin sharing our pains, joys, and challenges with one other. We need to stop feeling ashamed of our experiences, no matter how awful they may seem, and we must stop judging. We need to work to discover how to command respect—from our families and spouses, from our communities and colleagues. It's only by talking, by considering, by opening our eyes, hearts, and minds that we can control our own destinies. But like everything in life, this is a decision that *you* have to make. Be prepared to take a journey of self-discovery and self-love, and know that ultimately, you, too, can create your own self-fulfilling prophecies. *¡Adelante mujer!* You go, girl!

1 THIS IS MY LIFE

When asked to describe myself, I always answer that I am an empowered Latina, a woman who knows that she can provide for herself financially, emotionally, and spiritually. I am proud not just of who I am, but also of the *process* of becoming who I am.

As a businesswoman and professional, an educator, a member of numerous community boards, and a mother, I may not appear to be someone who has been through tragedy after tragedy. If you met me, you would never be able to guess what my life was like as a child and young adult. I've been knocked down over and over again, both literally and figuratively, but there is nothing in the world that can keep me down, because despite the odds, I've never allowed my soul to die.

There have certainly been times when I have fallen into the trap of giving my power away to various people and situations, especially because I'd been "trained" by my father and my culture to do so. I didn't know any other way; I didn't have the resources to help me find a better method of self-discovery. Now I have learned how to take care of myself, and more important, I know why it is absolutely necessary to put myself first.

I would like to share with you some aspects of my life, examples of the way I grew up, how I gave my power away, and how I reclaimed it. The rest of the book is about *you*. I hope that my story of survival and success will help you find the strength within yourself to take back your power and control the rest of your life.

An American Dream Poster Family

At the beginning, my parents' relationship was the stuff of romance novels. They met at the airport in Mexico City, where my mother had gone for vacation from her native Chihuahua. My father was a handsome commercial airline pilot, living in Quito, Ecuador. But after that brief encounter, they didn't see each other again—until they got married, four years later. During the intervening years, they wrote to each other constantly, with an occasional phone conversation in between. Pressured by the family, my mother got engaged to a doctor in Chihuahua, but the day before the wedding she ran away to Quito and married my father instead.

A year later they decided to leave Ecuador because they wanted better opportunities for themselves and the children they planned to have. They arrived in Los Angeles in 1969 with a grand total of $200 in their pockets but determined to realize that dream. Without knowing a word of English they began working in factories at a time when the American dream was attainable to anyone willing to work hard—educated or not. My father made $20 a week at a lumberyard; my mother $15 at a factory making plastic plates.

When my mother was eight months pregnant with her first child, Dad was horrified to learn that she wasn't allowed to sit down on the job. To get a few minutes' rest, she would pretend to need to use the bathroom. Employees, however, were allowed only four minutes maximum to relieve themselves. My furious father decided then and there that neither he nor his family would ever again work for someone else. He would not be disrespected by anyone again, he swore.

So in 1970, his entrepreneurial adventures began. With $700 of their savings, my father went to a wholesaler and purchased some stereos and radios. He took a blanket from home, set the merchandise on it, and stood in the vendor's line at the Azusa swap meet. He made $30 on his first day. He was the happiest man in the world. For a while he continued working in the lumberyard during the week and selling stereos at the swap meet on weekends. Shortly after I was born, in 1971, my father opened his first business, a record store named Discoteca Latina. Within five years, he had opened a retail electronics store and invested in a number of other business ventures.

By 1977 my father was a millionaire. In less than a decade he had gone from impoverished and vulnerable to wealthy and powerful. He had everything a man could ask for, including a faithful and hardworking wife and three beautiful daughters.

As with many daughters, my life was ruled by my father. He was king of his castle, and had reason to be proud of his own hard work. He insisted that his daughters be well educated, so we were sent to strict Catholic schools. We were expected to excel, which we all did. We never disobeyed Dad, a strict disciplinarian who used both words and fists to impose his will on us—just as his own father had done. We took lessons in everything, from ice-skating and baton twirling to ballet and piano. We had so many classes and activities that my older sister developed stomach ulcers from the incredible pressure to perform. Although it could be frightening, I managed to cope, mostly because I simply believed that our lifestyle was normal, and everyone around us confirmed that.

We enjoyed (if you could call it that) luxurious surroundings and expensive baubles, given to us by a man who would build us up one day and break us down the next. We lived under his complete control (except for the times Mom covered for us), and it was his mission for his daughters to be both respected and respectable. Because he'd created us, he felt that he owned us. He tried to protect us from the dysfunctions of the world, yet he actively cultivated dysfunction in our own home through his fits of rage that stemmed from his alcoholism, combined with lavish gift-giving—all of which existed behind the façade of a wonderful family man. I was proud of being my father's daughter—I did feel protected—but what I didn't realize was that my protector was also my abuser. I wasn't yet able to see that sometimes our most important influences are also our worst oppressors, and that is why we should never depend solely on anyone else to help us define ourselves.

My mother was the perfect wife—that is, in the way most macho Latino men consider "perfect," which means, for one thing, that she stayed quietly at home while he ran around having mistresses all over the country. He had numerous illegitimate children with many different women, yet he consistently denied their existence to my mother, my sisters, and me. We were the chosen ones. He took pride in us, his primary family. He obviously instilled fear in those other women, because no phone call ever came in the night from a strange, desperate woman in another state. I some-

how knew that my father had other women, but I didn't
dare question him, for fear of what he would do to me for
being disrespectful. Respect was a very twisted concept for
him. I remember my maternal grandmother would tell my
mother, "Let him be. He's a man, and men are of the
streets. After all, you have all you need." That was my first
impression of marriage. Once we reached a certain age, we
girls were allowed to talk only to other girls. We were punished if seen anywhere near boys. Dad believed that all men
wanted just one thing, and no man was going to get it from
one of his daughters. Instead, he promised and delivered
the reward of any material items we wanted, so that no
man would ever be able to impress us with money. Ironically, at the same time, he was luring countless women with
his own money, power, and status. I didn't realize it then,
but now I see that my father knew what he was doing. He
was preparing us for men like himself. He saw how money
and power wooed women and he blamed woman's wily nature. Most women just wanted the easy way out, he believed. I happily accepted my rewards, and I behaved like a
good and loyal daughter.

A Family Shattered

When I was fourteen years old, everything changed.
Our world as we knew it collapsed, and during the next
few years all I had been brought up to believe in, everything I thought I knew about family—responsibility, loyalty, and honesty—was turned on its head.

I was a freshman in high school at the time and my

sixteen-year-old older sister, Judy, was a junior. One day, after having endured our father's ongoing sexual abuse, she reported him to our school's authorities. They sent a social worker to our home and my father had to move out.

The picture-book American family was no more.

After my mother and father officially separated, my father warned us that although he would no longer be living with us, he would continue to command and direct our every move. And for the next six years he did. I was attending San Diego State University when Judy, who was then twenty-two, called me one night. Infuriated by what he perceived as a threat to his indomitable presence, Dad had threatened Judy's boyfriend with violence. Although she was conditioned to be frightened by my father's rage, she also allowed herself to be angry this time. She had had enough of the violence. Dad had always been a tyrant when it came to our dating lives. Doling out threats directed at any potential date and at us, he rationalized his behavior by claiming, again, that he was only trying to protect us. Behind his back, and with the consent of our mother, we managed to meet and date boys, and we honestly thought that eventually he would realize we were growing up and he would relinquish his control on us.

Instead, though, he turned on us after this particular incident and vowed to disown the family. He stopped taking our phone calls. My mother and I couldn't understand why he refused to speak to us; we thought the trouble had been between him and Judy. We were wrong. I tried to contact him on a daily basis, but his employees had been instructed to tell us that he had nothing to say. Even my younger sister, Karina, who was twelve, tried to call him, only to be disappointed. He shoved the proverbial knife in deeper when he completely stopped providing for us financially. We'd always depended on him, and his abrupt actions left us in financial as well as emotional chaos. We were threatened with the loss of our home, our cars, and our dignity in one fell swoop.

Within the next three weeks, my mother was hospitalized after suffering a nervous breakdown, and Karina was notified by the private school she was attending that unless the past-due tuition was paid, she would not be able to return. Judy, the only one of us with a steady income, gave every last penny trying to save our home. My own part-time job funded my food and utility expenses, but not my rent or tuition. Our situation seemed totally hopeless. Then, as the weeks went by and we gathered what was left of our emotional strength, in a miracle of spirit we decided to fight back. The contract my parents had drawn up upon their separation stated that if, at any time, my father stopped providing for us financially, his businesses would automatically be transferred back to my mother. We knew that Dad was breaking the law, and Judy knew it was imperative that we hire an attorney and take Dad to court, a difficult mission without any money. We found an attorney who was willing to accept the case, with the provision that his fees be paid immediately upon the sale of our house.

On Christmas Eve of 1991, one of the most frightening days of our lives, we took legal action against the man we had always counted on, always trusted to protect us, and—although it was often difficult—always loved. We never thought we'd have found the courage, but with our very survival at stake, there was no other choice. Of the three sisters, the judge asked only Judy to enter the courtroom to testify. She walked straight to the witness stand, focused on Mom's face, and never glancing at Dad, she answered questions about the burden of instant and unexpected financial responsibility. When Dad took the stand, Judy dared to look at him—and, she said later, sadness swept over her. He had allowed his pride and machismo to take things too far.

When Mom walked out and shakily declared that the judge had ruled in our favor, we were ecstatic. We were temporarily granted 70 percent of the family businesses until a future court hearing. Dad was given two hours on the twenty-fourth of December and two hours on the twenty-fifth to remove his personal belongings from the business sites awarded to us.

We spent that Christmas Eve in the main shop, protecting the merchandise still left. Judy's boyfriend, Conrad, and mine, Joe, were there with us for moral and physical support. We feared that my father would return for some sort of vengeance. He had vowed to kill us if we ever antagonized him; taking him to court seemed far beyond that threshold. The next morning, Christmas Day, he came with one of his mistresses and illegitimate children to collect his personal belongings. With tensions as high as they were, it was no surprise that a fight erupted between Dad and Judy's boyfriend, and they beat each other brutally in the back alley. My father's business partner suddenly appeared with a gun, and in order to protect my father, he shot bullets in our direction. I jumped to cover up Karina, and we all rushed inside the store, where my boyfriend grabbed the business gun and ran back out, looking for Dad and his partner.

Not long afterward, a police helicopter began hovering over the scene, and crime unit officers arrived by the truckload. Six streets were blocked off while they searched for Dad. Within an hour, he was found hiding behind a house and was arrested. As he stood there waiting for the officer to open the back door of the car, he looked over at my mother, sisters, and me—the family he had created— with nothing less than hate in his eyes. Although we were surrounded by fifty police officers, we were terrified, certain that he would explode, knowing that as soon as he had the chance, he would kill us all. We had to be prepared to fight back.

The court charged my father as an accessory to attempted murder, but later dropped the charges because of a lack of evidence. After being released, Dad had the police drop him off right in front of our shop. He wanted us to see him and for us to know that we hadn't won.

Miracle at Rocky Bottom

From the day Dad disowned us until January 1992, I felt numb. I needed to be strong, though, not only for myself but also for the emotional and physical benefit of my family. We had survived months of what seemed like torture, and I thought I was ready to start my life again. Unfortunately, I was mistaken. I still had many hurdles to overcome.

One day in February, I woke up early for school, but when I tried to get out of bed, I felt paralyzed. My body wouldn't move. I had absolutely no physical strength. When I tried to lift my head, it hurt. I tried to raise my leg, and pain shot through it. I began to lift my arm, but it felt so heavy that it fell back down onto the bed. I lay there ter-rified. I used the bit of energy I had to sit up as feelings of desperation washed over me. I wanted to scream for help, but to whom would I scream? I knew I wasn't paralyzed; my muscles would grudgingly respond if I tried hard enough.

It took me three hours to leave the house that morn-ing, when it usually took me thirty minutes. I cried in frus-tration and pain. Getting through the next few days was miserable. I dragged myself out of bed in the morning and I cried in the shower. I cried because I hurt; I cried because the only time I didn't hurt was when I was sleeping. A few days later, anxiety and panic descended on me. I was so physically exhausted I had trouble making it to class. I had no interest in socializing with my friends or attending par-ties and events. No one seemed to understand me and I can't count the times I heard, "Just get up! Stop being so lazy!"

Lazy! I wish I had been just lazy. I couldn't even walk around school without crying, my body hurt so much. I de-cided to seek help and went to a university psychologist. I spilled my guts about the events of the past few months and was immediately diagnosed with post-traumatic stress disorder (PTSD). Everything I had experienced had wreaked havoc on my mind and body. The doctor told me there was nothing I could do but let it play itself out, and with time the effects would go away. I wish I'd known then to find a better doctor.

For five months I lived in misery. When I was alone in my apartment, I turned off all the lights, disconnected the phone, and cried for hours. I didn't know why I was cry-ing, really, but I remember the pain of feeling as though my heart were being ripped apart. My friends began to worry about me and would visit just to cheer me up, but I had no interest. I felt as if my soul had been shattered. I couldn't find the physical or mental strength to pick up the pieces and put them back together again. As summer came, my depression worsened, seriously compromising my full-time summer job. I needed to work to survive, but physically I could no longer function.

All of my life I had been against drugs. Friends of mine used them, but they knew not to offer me any. But on July 3, 1992 (I'll never forget that date), I was lying in bed, feeling as though I couldn't handle another day. I had attempted to see doctors, but without insurance I couldn't afford the endless sixty-dollar office visits, let alone the prescription costs. Although I felt severely depressed, collapsing was not an option. My mother had just been released from the hospital, and Judy had finally reached the end of her rope as well, taking off from work for emotional distress. Meanwhile, Karina was desperately in need of the mothering that our mother could no longer provide.

I gave myself two options. Either I could lie in bed and hope to die, or I could do whatever it took to make myself get up, go to work, and function as a sister, daughter, employee, and student. I chose the latter and began to take methamphetamine, also known as speed, in order to medicate myself.

"Since when do you use speed?" my friend Michelle asked when I begged her to go with me to a former classmate's house to make my first purchase.

I was adamant. "Don't ask, don't advise, don't lecture. I have to do this. Please just come and get me and we'll go."

When we arrived at a bungalow, a woman shook out

what looked like a teeny amount of white crystalline powder on a mirror and lined it up with a credit card. I looked at the line and knew I needed it. I wanted it to survive. I took the straw, snorted the line, and within seconds, I felt something amazing. I felt as if I were coming out of a haze, as if I'd had shock treatment. I was on top of the world. I felt all-powerful, ready to take on anything, anyone. I convinced myself that I was going to use speed only to get over these tough times. Little did I know then that speed would nearly destroy my life. In no time, I was hooked. I did it in the morning, afternoon, and evening. I did it to go to work, and I did it to stay up at night. I knew it was wrong, but it gave me the false sense that I had control over my life, and that was exactly what I craved.

Before the ordeal of the past few months had begun, I had applied as a transfer student to the University of Southern California (USC). I received a letter from USC granting admission, along with a full financial-aid package consisting of grants and loans. There was no way that I could pass up the opportunity to attend one of the most prestigious universities in the country. Although I knew I was in no shape emotionally to take on this new challenge, in my eyes, education meant salvation.

In September of 1992, I began my new life at USC. Only Judy and a few friends knew that I was using speed. It wasn't difficult for me to play it off, because to the outside world I had everything together. Anyone involved in my drug use was completely dissociated from campus life. My roommate, George, had transferred with me from San Diego State—we had been friends for years. Despite our closeness, however, he didn't suspect for a minute that I was on drugs. My room was connected to a bathroom, so every morning it was easy for me to privately do a line of speed to numb my feelings of worthlessness. Then I'd walk out of my room, meet George at the front door, and walk to school to our first class. George knew that I had gone through serious family problems and admired me for staying so strong. To him, I was the same Yasmin he had known for years. I'd head home after classes and do another line so that I'd have the energy to study, staying up until three or four o'clock in the morning, reading things over and over, and often forgetting what I had just read.

After a few days, I got a job in a career services office. Completely numb to my pain and desperation, I was able to deal with my new school, my new job, and my new life with what I mistook for relative ease. Nonetheless, despite the new job, my sense of self-worth was completely shattered. How had I become so weak? How could I, someone people admired for abstaining all these years, become reliant on illegal street drugs? This sense of vulnerability was so emotionally intolerable to me that I could not discuss my drug use with anyone except those who already knew. So I continued to live my life as a closet user and convinced myself that I would stop using speed during Christmas vacation, when I didn't have to go to school and I could sleep it off. When December came along, I went to my mom's and was determined to rest and sleep and do whatever it took to stop using speed.

From December 21 through December 24, I slept and slept, comforted by the idea that I had made it through the rough times and that my body and mind would be ready to go back to normal. On December 25, I woke up, sure that I had slept enough and that I would feel good, but I was wrong. All the feelings of insecurity and hopelessness that I had experienced before I started doing speed came back with a ferocious intensity. Once again I became utterly immobilized. It took less than ten seconds for me to make the decision: I ran to the bathroom and did a line. This time was different, though. I was terrified, knowing now that I no longer controlled the drug; the drug controlled me. I wanted to stop. I really wanted to stop, but I couldn't. I had become an addict.

In January 1993, I returned to school in worse shape than ever. Feeling out of control only made me want to do more speed. I figured that the more I did, the better I would feel. But the more I did, the worse I felt. As much as I tried to get the powerful feeling back, I couldn't. I didn't know where to go; I didn't know who to turn to. I was so ashamed—I felt like a fake. Was I the strong, powerful woman who could handle it all? Or was I a weakling who couldn't even get out of bed in the morning to face the day?

By March, I was often too sick to go to work and I was missing more and more classes. Soon after, I told my boss I had to quit. I took some diamond jewelry that my father had given me and pawned it for $600. I figured that this money would serve as a substitute for my work income until the end of the semester. When the end of the semester came along, I did nothing but cry. I cried out of desperation, cried out of depression, cried because my life was worse than it had ever been. When it was time for finals, I couldn't make it to class without breaking down. On the day of my accounting final, I was so depressed and physically weak that I didn't even show up. The next day, I went to see my professor. He took one look at me and told me not to worry. He wasn't going to make me take the final— he would just assign a final grade on the work I had already done. He certainly didn't know that I had destroyed myself doing speed; he just took one long look at me and knew that something was terribly wrong.

Between January and June of 1993, I secretly and frantically looked for professional help. But without health insurance, I couldn't afford anything but a free counseling session. I'd never been aware of how devastating life was for those who could not afford health insurance. I was crying out for help, but I couldn't get anyone to listen. "Can't you see?" I begged so often. "I need help. I'm not asking for free help. I will pay you once I graduate. I only have eighteen months until I graduate with a business degree from USC, and I will start making payments with my first paycheck."

"Sorry," they'd all reply. "We don't have any loan programs. The only way you can go into rehabilitation is through private health insurance or state-provided Medi-Cal." Medi-Cal had never even occurred to me. Maybe there was some hope after all. I would simply go to the state and ask them for temporary help with health insurance. How could they refuse someone in my position? I went to the Los Angeles County Social Services Center and filled out what seemed like two dozen forms. I sat there for most of the day waiting for them to call my name. Finally, six hours later, it was my turn.

"Are you pregnant?" the clerk asked, bored.

"No, no," I said.

"Are you under the age of eighteen?"

"No."

"Then there is nothing we can do for you."

I was dumbstruck. "But I'm a student who desperately needs some help. Isn't there any way the state can help me?"

"Only if you're pregnant or a minor." The clerk turned on her heel, done with me. I had been under the impression that it was a good thing to go to college and not get pregnant, but in my case, I would have been better off knocked up.

By the end of May, my depression had deepened and I had become manic. I remember watching Oprah's show and desperately wanting to write her a letter because I honored and respected her for being a survivor. I related to her, and she brought me comfort. When she talked about her life, I truly felt her pain, and in the core of my soul, I believed that I still had some hope for survival—one day I, too, could become the successful woman I had always wanted to be. I didn't heed that soul tug then, though. Instead, in one of my very frequent moments of cynicism and hopelessness, I thought about it again and decided not to write the letter. I knew there were probably thousands of people who wrote her letters asking for help. What made my situation any different?

By the time the semester ended, the drugs had overtaken my immune system, and it took me three times as long to do even the simplest tasks, like packing and moving out. The situation with my family had gotten worse. We'd lost our house and had only a few weeks to find somewhere to live. Because I was still maintaining impossibly high expectations for myself, I had applied for a summer internship at the McDonald's Corporation, was awarded the position, and was to begin my corporate training the first week of June. The night before my first day of work, I couldn't sleep. I was, understandably, nervous about being able to function normally at the job, and terrified that management would be able to tell I was high.

All night, I waited for the clock to read 5:00 AM so I could get up and get ready. I was so afraid that I might oversleep and be late my first day that I didn't sleep at all. At 6:30 AM, I began driving up the freeway. The lack of sleep and my manic episodes had reached a peak, and I begged God to please just let me die. "Just let my car malfunction and wreck. I'm done. I can't take it anymore," I prayed out loud. I didn't have the courage to take my own life, but I was telling God that I would rather die than continue living in misery. I had finally hit rock bottom. There was no more "pulling through" or overcoming anything. My life was no longer worth living. I was completely exhausted, physically, emotionally, spiritually.

Whether by the grace of God or by my own last unconscious wish to survive, I pulled off the freeway. Within feet was a pay phone. In a state of fogginess, I got out of the car, shaking. I had no idea what I was doing, but I got out and walked to the phone. The first thing I saw was a sticker with the number of a suicide hotline pasted to the metal casing. Barely readable—written over with graffiti and adorned with old chewing gum and other sticky substances—the suicide hotline number nevertheless jumped at me. I dialed it. "Disconnected," a recording told me. "God help me, God help me, God help me," I kept repeating. I rummaged through my wallet and found the number of a rehabilitation clinic. They kept me on hold for twenty minutes while I watched cars whizzing by, full of people who had a life, who had hope, who had a plan. Twenty minutes felt like twenty hours. I hung up and went back to my wallet, searching through business cards and numbers written on torn pieces of paper, resources that had all turned me down over and over again. Two-thirds of the way through my useless stack of so-called people to turn to, I found the home number of Laura, a therapist whom I had spoken with by phone at the Beverly Hills Women's Clinic. After having been turned down so many times, I had regarded her kind words—like those of so many others—with cynicism. Oddly, though, I remembered that she had given me her home number that day, although it was against the rules. It was 6:55 in the morning when I called her.

"Who is it?" she answered.

"It's Yasmin," I said, shaky and feeling as if anything I said would come out like gibberish. "I spoke to you over the phone awhile back. You gave me your home number in case of an emergency . . . I'm sorry to bother you, but I don't know who else to call. I need help so badly . . . Please help me!" I was sobbing so hard I could barely speak. "I don't want to live like this anymore. I'd rather die. Please, Laura, help me."

She was silent for a few seconds, took a deep breath, and told me, "For the past seven years I have been teaching yoga at six AM every morning, and I've never missed a class. But something strange happened this morning. My alarm clock didn't go off. I know I set it last night. This morning I could not understand why my alarm didn't ring, but now I do understand. If it had gone off as it always does, I would not have been here to answer your call." I knew down deep in my heart that this was no coincidence. "Where are you? Stay put. I'll be right there."

I had never felt God's presence as deeply as I had at that moment. For the first time in my life, I had experienced a true miracle. I did not know this woman. I had never even met her, but I knew God had intervened so that she could help me. She arrived within fifteen minutes and

took me to the clinic. We searched through the clinic refer-
ences for eight hours, calling many rehabilitation centers
and asking them to take me in. "No insurance, no money,
no service" is what one clinician told us. Finally, we found
a center that was willing to give me a five-thousand-dollar
loan.

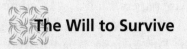 The Will to Survive

On June 12, the day before I was to enter the recovery
center, I was extremely anxious. I knew I was going to get
better, but I was also terrified. That night, my family had
a college graduation celebration for Judy. Although my
friends and family surrounded me, I felt totally alone and
detached. While they sat around the table, happily laughing
and talking, I prayed to God that one day I could be happy
again. My mother instinctively knew something was very
wrong with me and would have been horrified by the truth.
Before I went to bed, I went to her room and told her,
"*Mami,* I need to go away for a while. I need to deal with
what's happened to me because of Dad. I'll be back in a
few weeks." She didn't really understand what I was talking about, but she comforted me and told me she loved me.
She made me chamomile tea and held me in her arms until
I fell asleep.

The next morning, I awoke from a half sleep at five.
I packed my things and woke Judy, who had offered to
drive me to the recovery center in Laguna Beach. I thought
we had somehow made a mistake when we reached the
address that I had written down. Instead of the cold, in-

timidating institution I had pictured in my mind, we were in the driveway of a beautiful mansion surrounded by flowers and greenery, with a breathtaking view of the Pacific Ocean. First Step, which had only opened within the past few months, had been founded, and funded, by a wealthy businessman whose brother had died from a heroin overdose. I couldn't believe how blessed I was to have found Laura and this program. Judy checked me in and signed all of the loan papers, and I was admitted. Now, nothing mattered. All I wanted was to feel safe, nurtured, and taken care of. For so long I had played this nightmare of a game, and it was finally over. I slept fourteen hours the first night there.

Rehabilitation was nothing like what I thought it would be. There were only nine residents, in for a range of addictions from alcohol to heroin, speed to marijuana. A staff of doctors and counselors was on hand twenty-four hours a day. One patient was the CEO of a Fortune 500 company; another was a sixteen-year-old trying to kick a heroin habit. Some people truly wanted to be there; others had been forced to go by the court. It was immediately apparent that drugs cross all economic and ethnic lines and that the rich just do more expensive drugs, while the poor do whatever they can get. After I'd spent forty days at First Step, my counselors and I felt that I was ready to go home and begin a new life. I started working two weeks after I left the center, and shortly after that, I began the fall semester at USC. My friends asked, "How was your summer?" And I could only answer, "Full of life-changing experiences."

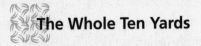

The Whole Ten Yards

By the fall of 1993, my life was to take another big turn, fanfares and fireworks included. This time the turn was for the good, at least for a while.

Although I'd vowed, when I started college at the University of Southern California in 1992, that I would never date a football player, I met Norberto Garrido in 1993, when we both lived within a few blocks of the university. Later, thanks to mutual matchmaking friends, we ended up swapping phone numbers, and slowly but surely developed a relationship.

In October 1994, my friends and I went to the Coliseum for the annual USC versus Oregon State football game. All week, my friends had been calling to make sure I would attend, something that was a bit odd since I rarely missed a game. On game day, just after the end of the fourth quarter, with sixty thousand people in the stands, the USC marching band began to play the wedding march. Someone told me to look over at the scoreboard—where big bright letters read: YASMIN, I LOVE YOU. WILL YOU MARRY ME? Then actual fireworks started to burst above my head. My friends walked me down to the field, where Norberto was waiting for me with my engagement ring. Security guided me to the center of the field; Norberto got down on one knee, told me how much he loved me, and asked me to spend the rest of my life with him. I was astonished. I looked up and saw thousands of people cheering us on, screaming, "Say yes! Say yes!" I looked over at the big stadium TV screens and saw my tear-streaked face. Never in my wildest dreams had I imagined that my marriage proposal would be like this. Norberto was too shy, or so I thought! I said yes, and he slipped the ring on my finger. We got married a few months later.

In 1996, the USC football team won the division championship and clobbered Northwestern University at the Rose Bowl. Having graduated the previous year, I was working for Philip Morris, and Norberto and I were very happy. Everything seemed perfect! Life was full of promises. Norberto was drafted by the National Football League; his dream had finally come true and we happily anticipated a new life of fame, fortune, and unforgettable moments.

However, it didn't take me long to find out that although the NFL does offer all of the above, it comes at a very high price, a price I was not willing to pay. Instead of taking me forward in time, life as an NFL wife took me back to situations and ways of thinking that I had worked very hard to avoid. I was expected to devote every moment of my time and every iota of my energy to my husband. I had never lived in anyone's shadow! Instead, I had struggled to overcome the difficulties that life threw in my path. I thought I was now free to live the life I chose, but in the NFL there are no choices—either you're in or you're out. Players and their wives must play by team rules and by those rules alone. The fact is, if you don't like the rules, there is always someone dying to take your place. My husband needed my support, and I knew how much this meant to him, so I had two choices: learn to play the role of an NFL wife or create a role for myself in which I could offer support to Norberto without sacrificing my soul doing it.

The expectations of an NFL wife and the expectations of a traditional Latina wife mirror each other in an uncanny way. Wives in both arenas are expected to be very traditional. Contrary to what most people think, NFL wives rarely have nannies to take care of their children or a cleaning staff to take care of their home. It's not that the wives can't afford help; it's that, in the world of the NFL, value is placed on a wife who takes care of her own children and home.

In April 1996, Norberto was drafted by the Carolina Panthers, and we moved to Charlotte, North Carolina, that summer. The first thing I noticed when I arrived was that there were no Latinos in sight. Fortunately, since my husband was in football camp, I had brought my mother and a friend along to help me get settled. The second thing I noticed: there were no corn tortillas anywhere, and my mother couldn't find her favorite newspaper, *La Opinión*.

Two weeks later, my mother and friend left, and my husband came home. From that day forward, everything changed. He seemed different—distant and detached. I had no idea at the time that this was the norm for many NFL players. Just as Latina mothers told their daughters, "Don't bother your dad; he's tired from work," NFL wives were not supposed to "bother" their husbands during football season. I tried to blow off his behavior as stress from the demands of professional football.

The more time that went by, however, the more distant my husband became. I tried to adjust to the lifestyle, going to the Panthers' Wives Association meetings and to all the charity events the wives attended. The problem was, I felt empty and objectified. I was no longer perceived as Yasmin—the young woman with immense goals and aspirations. I was just a "Panther wife." No one seemed to be interested in my life and dreams; all they wanted to talk about was my husband and football. When I tried to reach out and create my own identity in this new town, I was ostracized and told that I wanted too much in life, that I just needed to have babies, and then all that energy I had for life would diminish. The more I tried to find commonalities between the other wives and myself, the more I realized how different we were. When we all got together, talk revolved only around our husbands. In fact, I got to know more about these women's husbands than about them!

As the season continued, my husband became more and more arrogant. The whole town praised these guys as if they were gods. I began to understand why so many young NFL players get themselves into serious trouble; when you take a twenty-one-year-old boy who hasn't yet established his own identity and give him a few million dollars and treat him like a god, sooner or later he starts to believe he is somewhat like a god.

It wasn't long before I felt completely confused and alone. I couldn't find anyone to turn to for support, because everyone thought I had it so good. When I tried to discuss my situation with friends and family, they just did not seem to understand. "Problems? You don't have problems. I wish I had your problems instead of mine" is what one friend told me. No one could see the situation through my eyes. It wasn't about the money; it was about my soul dying a little bit each day. I always had the choice to leave North Carolina, but I believed that the man I had fallen in love with still existed, and I would get him back. Clearly, though, the price I was paying was taking an emotional toll on me. I had survived so much, and I had obtained a good education in order to have a great career and live my dreams, but that didn't seem to matter anymore; there was no room for my dreams in the NFL. I supported my husband's decision to join the NFL, and I loved him for who he was, but if he was no longer going to be the man I'd known before he entered the NFL, then he was no longer going to be my husband.

Although my husband was very *verbally* supportive, he was becoming less and less emotionally available to our marriage. Back in Los Angeles during the off-season, we saw a marriage counselor who tried to help us work through our problems. Norberto learned that a marriage is not something you can check in and check out of. He learned that constant communication and emotional availability are crucial if you want your marriage to work. He began to communicate with me more effectively, and finally, after two years of emotional turmoil, I found new hope.

The newfound but, as it turned out, temporary harmony in our marriage came to wonderful fruition with the birth of our daughter, Divina, on September 8, 1999. Shortly thereafter, I began work on my first book.

Eventually, despite our attempts to make things work, it became clear that our relationship was beyond repair. My husband and I had grown apart emotionally. I had spent the eight years we'd been together seeking personal growth, he hadn't. We were on different emotional levels and could no longer relate to each other. I had learned that unless both parties in a marriage grow together, one will be left behind. We had reached a point where we were truly in different worlds. I craved and needed an emotional connection with my husband—a connection that was no longer possible.

Although it was my decision to end the marriage,

there was emptiness inside my soul. The end of my marriage was not only the end of an institutionalized union, it was the end of a dream, a dream I'd had for most of my life: to marry a man I loved deeply and wanted to be with forever. My divorce represented a loss of myself: the self that had chosen Norberto as the man I would be with for the rest of my life. I felt betrayed by my own self. How could my love for my husband have changed so much? Could I even trust my own instincts anymore? I felt as if I had lost the trust of my heart and feared that I might never be able to love one man forever.

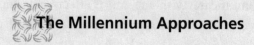 ## The Millennium Approaches

Since my last few years of graduate school at the end of the 1990s, I had been studying and researching the subject of Latinas and the cultural barriers we face, and solutions for overcoming them. I found very little that had been published on this topic, so I began to gather materials and interviewed hundreds of Latinas willing to share their stories. From this amazing process, which was central to my own recovery, a book emerged: *Empowering Latinas— Breaking Boundaries, Freeing Lives*. It was published in October 2001.

I dedicated the book to my husband, thanking him for teaching me what a real man was all about. There was a picture of my husband, daughter, and me as a happy family in the beginning of the book. Yet at the time the book came out, of course, we were not a happy family. In fact, Norberto and I had officially separated two weeks before the book's debut. But he showed up at the first book signing and we played it off as if everything were fine. The last thing I needed was for the focus to be on my failing marriage.

The response to the book was phenomenal. From January through July 2002, I was on a national book tour, trying to break new ground and find my new life as a single mother and a single woman. Although it was great, I was very lonely. I don't know what I wanted—maybe I didn't know what I was lonely about. Maybe I mourned for the loss of my marriage. But the success of the book, and the positive impact it was having on women I met along the way, centered my life, gave me new strength, and replenished my reservoir of hope.

Then the summer crashed into another family tragedy.

On August 11, Norberto, who by then was my ex-husband, pulled up into my driveway. He came in and said, "Yasmin, please sit down. I have something to tell you." At first I thought something had happened to Divina, who had been spending the weekend with him. But he reassured me that she was fine at his parents' house. He sat next to me, looked straight into my eyes, and said, "There was an accident . . . and Karina, your baby sister, is gone."

"What are you talking about, Karina is gone?" I asked in disbelief.

"She was hit by a drunk driver and she didn't make it," he said.

"No, this is not true. There is no way!" I yelled. "No, I need to talk to my sister Judy, now . . . I need to talk to Judy now!" I pleaded.

Norberto picked up the phone, dialed Judy's number, and gave me the phone.

"Please, Judy, tell me it's not true, tell me it's not true," I cried.

"I'm sorry, sister," she said. "It's true, Karina is gone. She's gone."

I cried with the deepest anguish I had ever felt. "God, why? Haven't we been through enough?" I screamed. Judy had been at the scene of the accident; she had seen it all. She had been in the car with her boyfriend while my baby sister and her friend Garthea followed them. Judy was looking through the rearview mirror when she saw a van ram the side of Karina's car. Judy ran to save my sister, but when she approached the wreckage, Karina and Garthea were not alive. They had died on impact.

That was the worst day of my life. I tried to be strong. I told myself, *"Everything happens for a reason*—NO! *Tragedies only make you stronger*—NO!" None of the mantras that had helped me in the past were working. I didn't care about *why* this happened; I just wanted my sister back. I didn't care about "the lesson" this was supposed to teach me, or that I'd be "a better person" because of it. Bullshit.

Bullshit or not, I kept trying to get my life together and forge ahead with my projects. I had to. My livelihood depended on it, and so did my daughter's. My career depended on it, too. I was a single mother now, receiving only $300 a month from my ex-husband. That realization gave me the kick in the pants I needed to pull myself together.

A few days later I had to fly to Dallas to negotiate a contract with Ramiro, a private investor I had met a few months earlier. He believed in my business and felt that I could help change the lives of Latinas all over the world.

My business relationship with Ramiro continued to develop after the successful meeting. He believed that it was time to bring more players into the game to fund the growth of his "soon-to-be-superstar"—so he said. He gathered several other investors and flew them into Los Angeles to meet me. They seemed to be intrigued and impressed by something I said because by the end of the night, they were offering me the moon and the stars. "We will give you anything you want, Yasmin, if you sign an exclusivity contract with us," they told me.

"What does that mean?" I asked.

"It means that we will make you the most happening thing since sliced bread, but we will be the exclusive company handling all operations for your career. You just have to worry about being talented and we will take care of the rest."

"I don't know if I would want to do that," I said, "but if I did, I would need a personal assistant—my sister, Judy—to come work with me as vice president or something; my own offices; and thirty thousand dollars a month salary." I was just throwing things out there, not thinking for a minute that they were going to buy it.

"Okay," they said. "It's yours. Everything you asked for is yours in return for full control and operation of the Yasmin Davidds brand."

"Brand? What do you mean by brand?" I asked.

"We are going to convert you into a best-selling brand. You do need to understand that your life will no longer be yours; you will no longer own your time. You need to do whatever we believe needs to be done in order to increase the market value of the Yasmin Davidds brand."

"Oh no," I said. "I'm sorry, but my soul—or should

I say 'my brand'?—is not for sale. My life is my own, and the only way I am going to make sure I keep it that way is for me to keep ownership of it. Therefore, I decline your offer."

They were shocked! They could not believe that I was turning down what they considered to be the deal of a lifetime. For the next few days they continued to try and persuade me to take the deal, but I was not going to budge. "Fine," they said. "We will talk about the deal later; let's just get back to business." So without my signing anything with them, they willingly hired my sister as a vice president, got me a full-time personal assistant, gave me offices, and began paying me $30,000 a month.

The next six months were hideous. They hired supposed experts to "groom" me into becoming "a brand." "No red lipstick," the supposed experts told me. "We need to sell you to the white man, so we have to straighten your hair, give you a nude-color lipstick, and dress you in some neutral colors."

"But that does not represent who I am," I told them.

"We are the experts, Yasmin—let us do our job."

"You might be the experts for other people, but you are not the experts of me. I thought you were hired to take me to the next level of my career, not to change who I am," I said.

Little did I know that business deals were going on behind my back. These people had a vested interest in creating a "new me" because if they created me, then they believed they had a right to claim a certain percentage of my market worth. If they took who I was and took me to the next level, they would never be able to claim that they had "made" me, and therefore would make less money off me. Well, thank God for my stubbornness, because I refused to give in to their suggestions of who I should become. What they were requesting of me did not feel right, and if it did not feel right, then I wasn't going to do it.

It was August 2003 when Ramiro asked to meet with me for a private lunch. By now I was dedicating all of my time to this one project, fully depending on it financially. As I sat down for lunch with Ramiro, he handed me a document. "This is the contract we want you to sign. We need you to sign it within forty-eight hours. If you don't, we will no longer pay you or your staff your salaries."

"But my attorney is not even in town," I told him.

"You don't need an attorney for this," he said. "Don't you trust us? We've been investing hundreds of thousands of dollars into you and you are questioning our loyalty?"

"I don't sign anything without my attorney reviewing it first."

"Fine," he said, "but we need this signed within forty-eight hours. We cannot continue handing over money without a contract signed."

I went home, reviewed the contract, and almost fell to the floor. Were these people serious? Did they really believe I was going to sign a contract that would give them ownership of me? The deal that I had refused to accept six months ago was now fully outlined in the contract. The worst part of all is that they wanted all rights to me and my name. When the contract ended five years from now, I would have to *pay them* to use my own name. There was no way I could sign this. I faxed it over to my attorney, who was in another state, and he quickly called me. "Don't you dare sign this contract, Yasmin," he told me. "This contract is so bad, I could not represent you if you chose to sign it." I informed Ramiro that I would not be able to sign the contract. Twenty-four hours later, all funds for the project had been pulled.

That quickly, my sister, Judy; my personal assistant, Kathleen; and I were without income. I sat there and cried, not knowing what to do. I knew I couldn't sign that contract, yet I felt responsible for my sister and Kathleen; their livelihood depended on me. Not only that, I had gone from making $30,000 a month to zero, and I had only a little money saved.

We needed to move forward without the investors, so that is what we did. We had to literally start all over. It was hard, very hard, but we knew that somehow we had to start building some business. None of us had enough money to tide us over until "real" money came in to the business again.

That same week, I received a letter from the investors' attorneys telling me that unless I negotiated a deal with the investors or repaid the $1 million they had invested in me, they were going to sue me. I hired a group of attorneys who agreed to be compensated at the end of the deal. We planned conference-call meetings between my investors in Miami, their attorneys in New York City, and my attorneys and me in Los Angeles. The more conference calls we had, the farther away from a deal we got. As all of this was going on, my friend Genevive saw that I was really stressed. She came to me and said, "Yasmin, I have an investor friend who I think could help you. He is an expert in big-deal making. I want you to meet him."

When I Thought It Was Safe to Get Back in the Water . . .

With some reluctance I agreed to meet "Lionel." He seemed like a very interesting, intelligent man. I explained the situation, and he immediately said, "I think I can help you." Next thing I knew he was totally engulfed in making sure I was protected from the investors. I fired my attorneys and brought Lionel on as the middle man to negotiate the deal between my investors and me. He was smart and quick-witted, and his business tactics were impressive. One night, while having dinner at his home, Judy and I spoke about how much we missed our little sister. After Judy had gone home, Lionel came up to me and with the tender, most caring eyes a man could possibly have, he put his arms around me and said, "Don't worry, I am going to take care of you and make sure nothing bad ever happens to you. If you need to cry for your sister, you can cry in my arms. I promise you I will never let you go." For the first time in many years I felt safe, and it felt so good. Little did I know that another shark attack was about to take place.

Lionel and I became intimate. I needed love and understanding, and he provided that for me. I needed safety, and he gave that to me. I yearned to be nurtured, and he provided that, too. Until then, I had never understood why people went to extreme lengths to fulfill their most basic needs of love and safety. Now I was in that very same predicament.

At first, Lionel was my knight in shining armor. I thought he was an angel sent from heaven to help me. But as it turned out, he was a con artist. Over a period of three months he nearly destroyed my life. He preyed on my weaknesses and my need for love and safety. He was a brilliant man who was also deeply religious (in a very distorted way), giving as much as $500,000 to his church. But he became an expert at using his apparent religious devotion to manipulate me.

At first, negotiations with the investors went great. Although my investors and I had been through a lot together, they trusted Lionel because I had brought him in to do business with us. But after a few meetings I noticed my investors pulling away. They knew something was not right with their dealings with Lionel. I knew it, too—well, I kind of knew it but would not admit it to myself. It's interesting how our psyches work. We lie to ourselves and convince ourselves that something is true even when the untruth of it is staring us in the face. And that is exactly what I did. I convinced myself of so many things to make the picture look right, yet every day I felt more and more powerless. Within three months, the investors pulled out of the deal completely, I had no money left, and I was three months late with my mortgage payments. I was about to lose my home.

It was November of 2003, and I was an emotional mess. "God, I have no idea what is going on here. All I know is that if empowering people is not my purpose in life, I can live with that. You just need to show me that there is no way out this time, and I will switch careers. Only a miracle from you can make me keep going." I went to sleep that night, not knowing what I was going to do or where I was going to live. The next morning I received a call from a dear friend, Robert. He knew the situation I was in and wanted to help me. "Yasmin," he said, "you cannot lose your house. Why don't you put your house up for sale and live off the profit for a while?"

"I wish I could do that, but my house is already in foreclosure," I said. "They will take it away before I can sell it." Robert arranged things so that I could acquire a twenty-thousand-dollar loan that I could pay back once I had sold my home. The next morning, I picked up the cashier's check, ran to my bank, cashed the check, and went straight to the mortgage company to pay my past-due mortgage payments.

The next day, my house went up for sale, and within four days it was sold. On December 29, 2003, I moved out of my home in Chino Hills. I had made $90,000 on the sale of my home, and after paying all the money I owed, I would have $60,000 to work with. I didn't know exactly which way I was going to take my business, but I knew that I had a financial cushion to carry me through the next few months until I figured it out.

By this time, Lionel and I were on bad terms. I had started to figure out that he was only out to get whatever he could from people in vulnerable positions.

On Three Kings Day, January 6, 2004, the remaining $60,000 from the sale of my home was wired into my business account. On January 7, 2004, I went to my bank to withdraw some money. "Sorry," the teller told me. "Your account is negative."

"Negative?" I said. "That can't be. I just had a sixty-thousand-dollar wire transferred into my account yesterday."

"Yes," she said, "I see that you did. But this morning, a Lionel Johnson cashed a check in the amount of sixty thousand dollars, leaving your account at a negative dollar and twenty-eight cents. It says that Mr. Lionel Johnson is a secondary account holder and is authorized to approve transactions on this account." My heart dropped. When Lionel and I started doing business together, we had opened a business account that allowed him to conduct business transactions, with my approval. He was my business partner, and that is what business partners do—they trust each other. I asked to see a copy of the check Lionel had cashed, and right there, in clear handwriting, was my signature—my forged signature. In the memo line of the check, he had written, "Joint investment funds." He had set me up, and now I was left with nothing—not even a dollar to my name.

The next morning, I was awakened by a call from the FBI. I was dumbfounded to find out that Lionel had been under investigation by the FBI, who had just arrested him that morning. The investigators wanted me to give a deposition of my business relationship with Lionel. I gladly granted them the deposition and vowed never to have any interaction with him again.

What was I to do now? How was I going to continue to run a business without any money? "Okay, God, this is it. I am tired. Please help me." A few days passed and I felt myself falling into a deep depression. I didn't want to see or talk to anyone. I was ashamed, ashamed that I had allowed this bastard to come into my life and turn it upside down. I had surrendered my power to him, and I was humiliated. I decided that I was going to start looking for other employment opportunities rather than pursue my business. I did not feel empowered at the time and I was not going to pretend that I was.

But my blessing continued and a few days later I received an email from L'eggs, the hosiery company. Management had done its research and decided I was the best fit to be the company's spokesperson for its Hispanic market campaign. The company offered me a significant amount of money just for the right to use my name, along with a one-year contract to travel around the country and represent L'eggs at top Latino events. I accepted the deal, and the launch of my new career began. The next twelve months were emotionally difficult because I had to come face-to-face with myself. It took me six months before I could truly talk about my experience. My close friends and family never judged me, always reminding me that I was human. Yet I believed that because I was an empowerment specialist, I had to be superhuman. It was when I faced my pain, my humanness, and my shame that I forgave myself and once again accepted myself—but this time with all my imperfections.

It was at that moment that I realized I had been asking God for the wrong thing. I had been asking God to bring back the old Yasmin, yet that was an impossible task. I realized that I had evolved to a whole new level, a whole new Yasmin. It was when I surrendered to myself and to God, accepting my faults and understanding that my imperfections were part of who I am, that I began to feel alive again.

I continue to walk my path, taking all of the risks necessary to live my life to the fullest and knowing that whatever happens, if I ever gave away my power again, I would always be able to reclaim it. Whether conscious or not, I gave my power away to life circumstances, yet when I was ready, I took it back. I am not an extraordinary woman with powerful gifts. I am a woman just like you.

A woman who has chosen to live her life with complete honesty, never being anything less than truthful to herself. If you live this way, you will always own your power. It is when you lie to yourself that you give away your power.

I am a true believer that whether we have been wronged, mistreated, screwed, or deceived, nothing we experience in life is accidental. Each situation is there to move us to the next level of awareness, of our true self. Our task is to figure out how this is true in our lives and to discover the gift that each event brings to our life. We grow and heal when we find the blessing in every event.

I have taken every tragedy and challenge in my life and have made it mean something to me in order to make sense of it. My depression taught me never to be ashamed of what I have gone through in life—everyone has a story to tell. My drug addiction taught me that unless I am emotionally well, I cannot take care of others, and the greatest gift a mother can give her child is her happiness. My father's mental illness and abuse taught me that unless I heal my pains of the past, they will come back to haunt me. My mother's pain taught me the value of economic independence and never to rely on one thing or person for my happiness. My sister's death taught me that life is too short for regrets, too pure for façades, and too deep for superficialities. It taught me that even if a part of me dies while I am alive, it is still possible to be reborn. My investors taught me that regardless of appearances, business is always business. My divorce taught me the value of being true to my spirit and living from my core. The betrayal of my business partner taught me that although vulnerability can be dangerous, it is never worth the closing of my heart.

Whether the meaning I have placed on these experiences is actually true is irrelevant. One thing I do know is that I will never suffer in vain. I will make sure that for every sorrow in my life, there is ten times the joy, and for every tear of grief I shed, there are a hundred tears of happiness.

I do not accept part-time love or part-time friends. When I love, I love passionately, with all that I am. If you ask my friends, they will say the same thing: that I live life in the present, and passionately. My life is more important than my career, and my daughter is more important than anything life has to offer. My mom, my sister, and my niece nourish my heart when I need love, and my friends fulfill my soul when it is empty. But at the core of my life lives faith: without God, nothing is possible.

 ## I'm Still Here

All of these lessons have given me the strength to thrive beyond chaos and live my life on purpose. For twenty years I had dreamed of having my own television talk show, one that would empower women from a Latina perspective. In October 2005, my dream came true when I launched *The Latina Perspective,* my weekly show in Los Angeles.

What else the future holds for me, I do not know. What I do know is that if life grants me joy, I will pass it on—and if it hands me grief, I will convert it into joy and then pass it on!

Meanwhile, I hope that the story of my life and the information in these pages will help you live your own life to the fullest, without regrets. Just as no one can tell me how to live my life, I would never tell you how to live your life. I can only help to guide you to your own truth.

Until next time, *¡hermanas!* I love you all, sisters!

2 WHERE HAVE ALL THE POWERS GONE?

Maybe I simply become whatever the man I am with wants me to be: "sex kitten," "controversial activist," "ladylike wife on the arm of corporate mogul." . . . Was I just a chameleon, and if so, how was it that a seemingly strong woman could so thoroughly and repeatedly lose herself? Or had I really lost myself?
—**Jane Fonda, quoted in Maureen Dowd's** *Are Men Necessary?*

What Is Power, Exactly?

Many women do not fully understand what power is—at least not the power I am talking about in this book. For some of us, power means getting someone else to do what we want him or her to do. This definition is often associated with things that women detest—maybe because way too often, we have been on the receiving end of power's effects: domination, authority, force, even violence. Then there is the other broad meaning of power: the ability or capacity to act. But power is much more than that. It is actually a resource. We can even say that it's like electricity. It's there, but unless you flip the switch, that vacuum cleaner is not going to slurp up the cat hair that's stuck to the rug; nor will that bedside lamp shed light so you won't trip and fall on your way to the bathroom in the middle of the night. We all have this natural resource inside, and we have the power to turn ourselves on.

Working with women, I have found that many of us are simply terrified to wield power. Women ask questions such as: "How do I let my power live inside me?" "Am I afraid of my power?" "Am I afraid of what it means to own my power?" These are valid questions. I see women of all ages and ethnicities searching for strength outside themselves. Many believe that a man or children or a house with a white picket fence will make their lives complete. A better job may make them happy. But to realize the best of ourselves—to turn on that flow of power within ourselves—we need a clearer understanding of just what "power" means. The lives we are living today are the consequences of the previous choices we have made. Owning our choices means owning our lives. This is the true meaning of power. The quality of our lives is determined by how much responsibility we are willing to take for the choices we make.

We can also see power as both external and internal. External power can be acquired through money, a career position, or the control of other individuals. I call this type of power "superficial power" because it can be taken away from us at any time. Internal power, or what I call "personal power," lives inside the core of our souls. It gives us the sense that there is nothing the world can throw at us that we can't handle. Internal power can't be given to us and it can't be taken away from us unless we allow someone, or something, to take it.

External power comes in many forms and influences us from the time we're children. We are often at the whim of our cultural traditions—shame, the fear of "what other people will say," institutionalized religion, and antiquated visions of what "good" women are supposed to be. We bend to our families and their often illogical and sometimes hurtful demands and desires. We long to please our bosses because we've been taught so well to please and to be cooperative at all times. We fantasize about money, handing our power over to the pursuit of material goods and the false respect that they bring. When a man enters our lives, too many of us lose ourselves, our unique personalities, our hopes and dreams. We give away every bit of our internal power to make someone else happy, or sometimes just to keep him calm.

In order to stop this outflow of power in its tracks, we need to look at the ways we allow such destructive processes to happen.

Giving Away Our Power Versus Surrendering

While I was waiting to go on a local television talk show in Miami to discuss the topic "Taking Back Your Power," the show's hostess mercifully interrupted me as I was about to munch on a calorie-loaded doughnut.

Monica wanted to go over a few things with me before we went on live. We sat on the sofa. "Yasmin, I would like to discuss a particular situation I'm sure our viewers would be very interested in," she said. "I know of a situation where a woman has a boss who makes her life miserable. He seems to feel threatened by this woman, and he is consistently setting her up for failure. None of his actions are outwardly visible to anyone else in the office, of course."

My first response was to ask Monica whether the woman had ever spoken to her boss about this situation. "Oh, yes," she answered, "but the boss denies everything. I feel terrible for her. The truth is, she's being tormented and she doesn't know what to do."

"Has she thought about leaving her job?" I asked, thinking it was an obvious question.

"Oh, no!" Monica said. "Then she'd really be giving her power away, wouldn't she? Then she'd be letting her boss win everything!"

"Honestly, I didn't realize this was a game."

"It isn't," she answered, confused.

"Then why is this woman treating it like one?" I asked. Monica couldn't answer. "Let me tell you something I learned a long time ago. This whole situation is not about the boss—this is about the woman in question. She is so worried about her boss, she's forgetting to take care of the most important person in her life: herself. She needs to make a decision based on what is best for her, not what is best for her ego."

Sometimes, out of a sense of injustice and outrage, we feel that we should not give an inch but instead should grit our teeth and stand our ground—or as I prefer to say, "stand on our power." But throughout the ups and downs of my life and career, I have learned that, sometimes, surrendering to a situation *is* standing in your power. On those occasions I exercised my power to pick my battles, because the truth is, certain situations are not worth our time and energy. It's up to you, however, to make the choice to let a situation go, and that is where your power comes into play.

You always have to choose whether to take action or surrender the situation over to the powers that be.

If the woman Monica described truly loves the company and the position she holds there, she would be wise and strong to do whatever it takes to work things out. This, however, does not mean that she should compromise her ethics or her personal power. If her boss makes her feel miserable, then she should report him to Human Resources. Regardless of the results, she'll end up gaining more power and self-esteem because she did what was right for her—she didn't allow anyone to infringe on her personal power. On the other hand, if she decides to stay in an uncomfortable situation because she doesn't want her boss to "win," it's too late. He's already wearing the victory crown.

There have been times when I have chosen to stay and fight for what I believed in, and at other times I have chosen to walk away. The most important insight I've gained from my experiences is that I derive my power not from any individual decisions I've made but from the realization that the decisions were mine and mine alone.

Power Zappers Versus Power Enhancers

The ability to plug into people who are power sources is a skill that enriches your life; allowing someone to short-circuit your life and drain your power is self-defeating. Power givers and power leeches are around us at all times. Learning how to distinguish between the two is essential.

There are three ways people behave when confronted by power in another individual:

- Some people support and nurture power in others, realizing that, especially for women, power is a positive and healing force.
- Others unintentionally or subconsciously chip away at that power.
- Then there are the leeches who intentionally and purposefully zap away at someone else's power.

A few years ago, I hired a manager to take care of my media appearances. Ironically, though, whenever I had an appearance, this person would become unbearably (and strangely) stressed out. It seemed that between managing the logistics and worrying about whether *I* would perform at my best, she turned into a basket case. Because I had already experienced so many years of unnecessary anxiety, however, I had mastered the idea that as long as I was "real," things would turn out exactly as they were meant to be.

I had been asked to appear as a guest expert on a major prime-time television show. The producer wanted to test me out, and if she liked what she saw, she was ready to work on getting me a regular spot. That morning, my mom had asked me if I was nervous.

"No," I answered, truthfully.

"But you're about to go on live TV in front of millions of people! How can you not be terrified?"

"I don't see it that way, *Mami,*" I answered. "I see myself as sitting down in a studio and having a conversation with some nice people who happen to be the hosts of this show. As long as I stay in my truth, I can't go wrong. If the producer likes me, then that's great. If she doesn't like what she sees, then that just means that particular show was not the right place for me to be." Mom thought about it for a second and then said, "You're right, *mijita*. You are absolutely right."

A few minutes later, my manager picked me up. The energy in the car was tense. "What's wrong, Michelle?" I asked. "Are you okay?"

"Yeah," she said in a tone that sounded like just the opposite. "We have to make sure we aren't late . . . and we have to make sure they do your hair and makeup right . . . and they'd better pronounce your name correctly," she snipped. "And, oh—whatever you do, make sure when you sit down, you cross your ankles and not your legs."

I was floored. "Is crossing my ankles that important, Michelle?" I asked as patiently as I could.

"Well, that's how all the women on TV do it. I've been watching, and they all cross their ankles; they don't cross their legs."

The whole conversation struck me as very strange. "But I'm not *all* the women, Michelle. Anyway, I don't like crossing my ankles; it's uncomfortable for me. I like crossing my legs." I assumed that was the end of the discussion.

Instead, she sighed in irritation and repeated, "Can you just cross your ankles, please?"

I looked at her with disbelief. "No, I can't. Not unless you can give me a valid reason why it's so damn important. Just because other women do it that way, that's not good enough." I wasn't done. "Now, if you tell me that crossing my legs gives some kind of negative impression on television, then I'll consider it, but you should know by now that I don't just follow the crowd to blend in nicely. That's not what I'm about."

"Fine," she finally grumbled. "But I don't know why you have to make things so difficult."

By the time we arrived at the studio, I felt as if all my positive energy had been sucked right out of me. Michelle had exposed me to unnecessary negativity, and my energy level had gone from brimming over to middling at best. Whether or not she'd meant to irritate me was irrelevant; the fact is, she had affected me deeply. Often, it makes no difference whether an action is intentional—the result is the same, and if we end up in a negative frame of mind, it's time to decide whether we should eliminate that source of negative energy.

The situation with my manager became too much to ignore in the days following the taping. My performance had been very powerful after all, and the producer asked me to be a regular on the show. Ironically, I had decided by that time that the show was not the right forum for me, so I politely declined the offer. Michelle was livid; she believed that the program was the opportunity of a lifetime. I knew then that I had no choice but to fire her. It was clear that Michelle was not there to serve *my* best interests. If she had ignored the dollar signs floating before her eyes and had taken the time to get to know me, she would have been aware from the beginning that to me, it's not about the destination but the journey. If she had listened to my message more carefully, she would have understood that the power of my career is in discovering my unique and powerful path.

I could not help comparing Michelle's reaction to that of my mother. *Mami* understood where my power was—in being myself—whereas Michelle, instead of nurturing that power, was willing to chip away at it to suit what she thought would please others.

The most insidious type of power zappers are the energy thieves. These are the most dangerous types of people to waste your time on, not because they may threaten you physically (that's a different topic entirely), but because they can leave you emotionally scarred for life. Sometimes, the worst energy thieves are all in the family. Most of us find it hard to accept that someone we know and love might be out to hurt us by robbing us of our most precious gift: our power. A person who tends to zap power doesn't necessarily have to be a malicious person—let me just phrase it more gently by calling such people disturbed and unable to tell right from wrong. These destructive types are always—without exception—burdened by their own issues, which almost never have anything to do with the person they are manipulating. Simply put, they cannot stand to see anyone else enjoy happiness because they are desperately unhappy themselves. Nevertheless, they still have the ability to hurt you if you let them; and when you allow others to hurt you, a piece of your spirit, the place where your power lives, shifts to their control. The good news is, this kind of power play is something you can learn to manage once you have the right tools. You will find them in subsequent chapters.

Family Power Versus Personal Power

Family loyalty above all else is a vital aspect of many cultures—and is especially important to Latinos. From early on, we are taught to be fiercely, unquestionably devoted to our families. Our parents never questioned this legacy—nor did our grandparents or their parents before them.

Let's face it: we have all done things that we knew were not practical, in our own best interests, or convenient—and that might even have been unethical—just because a family member asked us to do them. When asked why we did these things, we are not hard-pressed to come up with the answer: family comes before anything else. While I consider myself a very loyal person, I recognize that a decision made solely out of a need to be obedient, with no consideration for practicality, can be dangerous.

How we perceive power and relate to it determines how we interact with others throughout our lives. People who have been taught by their families to nurture their personal power grow into positive adults who demonstrate strength of character. These people make decisions from a position of power. Unfortunately, this is not the case for most women, who have seen their mothers, aunts, and sisters abandon their personal power to appease their men. Many of these women had their dreams and aspirations deflated at every step by their own mothers, who repeatedly pointed out their daughters' personal flaws: "You're too fat." "Your hair's too kinky." "Forget about college— you're not smart enough." As adults, women whose power was zapped in this manner will tend to make decisions from a position of weakness, which can only lead to an unhappy and unfulfilling life. We must make a concerted effort to help our sisters recognize the inherent passivity that certain aspects of our culture breed in women. By doing so, we can change these learned patterns of weakness and foster self-confidence.

How We Give Our Power Away to Men

Finding security through a man is a woman's greatest obstacle to keeping and maintaining her power. What I am talking about here is emotional security: the belief that you will be alone forever if you don't settle for that one man, even if he is less than what you want and deserve. The fear of being alone can drive even the strongest woman to sacrifice at least some of her personal power for emotional security. One surefire sign that this syndrome has overtaken a woman's better sense is when she begins to conform to what her man believes is right instead of standing up for her own beliefs. Another sign is when a woman begins to see herself through her man's critical eyes and she begins to spiral down into self-doubt, believing that her entire worth is in her appearance or her performance as a "good" girlfriend or wife. There is nothing wrong with compromise, but it ought to be fair and equal. In too many cases, women literally give up their power in order to be loved.

Melissa's story illustrates the kind of self-defeating, power-draining behavior that too many women engage in. What she didn't realize at the time was that sometimes when we lose something, we gain something much more powerful.

A few years ago I was at a very hip Latin-themed nightclub in Los Angeles. The place was filled with beautiful people dressed in thousand-dollar outfits and dripping with jewelry. I was having a blast, dancing to the pulsating beat with a few of my friends, both male and female, when I noticed a young woman crying in a corner. I could tell right away that she was a knockout, despite the black mascara running down her cheeks.

I walked over. "Honey, what's wrong?" I asked, putting my hand on her shoulder.

Sobbing, she was unable even to speak for a minute or two. "My boyfriend . . . he, he . . . we were here together and we were having fun. Then this woman came and whispered in his ear, and he just got up and he . . . he held her hand . . . and they started dancing." She buried her beautiful face in her hands. "I'm sorry. I don't mean to bother you."

"It's okay," I said. "I know you're really upset, and even though you don't know me, I promise you can trust me."

She hesitated for a moment and then broke out in fresh tears. "Now they're kissing! Right in front of me, I saw him kiss her—more than once! He's my boyfriend—why would he do this to me? Am I so bad, so ugly? Am I . . . nothing?"

I could see pure desperation in her eyes. I grasped her hand and forced her to look at me. "I want you to listen very carefully, girl. You do not deserve to be disrespected this way."

She pulled her hand away from mine and whispered, "But he's all I have. He makes me feel like I'm on this earth for some purpose, at least."

I knew I had to be as calm and reassuring as possible. "You don't need a man to make you feel good about yourself. You need to find your strength and confidence in your heart—inside of you—not from anyone else, especially some guy who conducts himself like a fool! If you depend on anyone else to tell you what you're worth, you will forever be confused and dependent. Look at you, girlfriend! You are stunning! You should be a respected queen!"

I continued, honestly, "There are a lot of beautiful women in this club tonight—some of the most gorgeous women in the world. But not all of them know what you know now. You are beautiful, but it's not just physical. You are beautiful deep down in your soul." I pointed to the crowd of so-called beautiful people, wondering to myself how many of these seemingly happy women were living under impossible limitations. "All women are born to be queens of their own destiny. We have ultimate power over our own thrones, our own kingdoms, and our own lives. We have absolute power over our own thoughts, actions, and beliefs. We alone choose how we will be treated." Then I asked her a question I hoped would hit home: "Would a queen allow a man to treat her the way your boyfriend has treated you tonight?"

She managed a smile and answered, "Not in a million years!" With what I knew was a renewed sense of hope, she threw her arms around me. "No one has ever said anything like that to me. Thank you for making me feel good, like I'm worth something—even if my man is a dog!" She had one more question for me, though: "Miss, you don't know me. Why did you take the time away from your friends to come over and ask me if I needed help? I'm just a stranger to you."

I'd heard the question before. "Because most of us just haven't figured out yet that we are powerful queens in our own right," I explained. "Instead, we act like servants so people will like us, and so we won't make waves. We end up forgetting that the most important person in our lives is us."

"A queen," she repeated back to me. "That sounds so conceited, though," she said, giggling.

"*Mija*, when I say queen, what I mean is a woman who recognizes her inner beauty and power and takes control of her own life. I know that most women have trouble viewing themselves that way, and that's because we've always been taught that our worth comes from the outside and what other people think of us. Society leads us to believe that our only measure of worth is what we do for others, not what we do for ourselves."

Out of the corner of my eye, I saw that my two male friends were watching our conversation. When they signaled for us to join them, I decided to bring my new friend with me—a decision I soon regretted when I saw that they were preparing to hit on her. As if demonstrating the points I had just taught her, these guys saw her as a lonely, vulnerable, easy target. Feigning concern, they asked if she needed anything. She shook her head and immediately turned her attention back to me, ignoring them completely. I was thrilled. Not only had my words hit home for her but they'd hit with record speed. Instead of turning to two ready and willing guys not three feet away, she wanted to keep talking about self-discovery and power.

"I need to tell you something," she said at the end of the night. "What you told me tonight will stay with me forever. I might have lost my man, but tonight I found myself."

Power is the strength and ability to see yourself through your own eyes and not through the eyes of another. It is being able to stand in your own power and not trying to take power from someone else. What this means is that you have defined your own values and your own truths—and you live them. You do not try to create your values and truth from someone else.

So what does power have to do with love? If you do not have personal power that includes love of self and others, it is tremendously difficult to maintain a happy life. I remember having a conversation with a colleague; she said that she thought happiness was overrated and momentary: "You have happy moments, yet there is no such thing as living a happy life."

"I completely disagree," I told her. "I know you could live a life of happiness, because I do. Sure, I have complicated and unpleasant situations in my life. I get stressed out, but I maintain a perspective that determines how I feel. I'm grateful for everything that comes into my life, even the bad. I know everything that happens is meant to teach me something, whether it's a demonstration of what works or of what doesn't work for me."

I went on to explain that when you see all of the events in your life as blessings, you can live only in a place of gratitude and happiness. If you can find the well of love that you have, and let it quench your emotional thirst, you will only end up stronger. Love, acceptance, and forgiveness are tonics for the soul. When we embrace love as a feeling *about* ourselves, *for* ourselves, it will never go away. When we understand that the love we feel is our own—not generated by a man or any other external force—then we see it differently. Power becomes an independent state of being that we maintain by keeping our hearts open.

Culture and the Media: Lies That Bind

How lucky our great-grandmothers were! They didn't have hundreds of television channels and dozens of women's magazines to show them that they looked all wrong. Today's pervasive media help shape our values, needs, and self-images. And that influence is not always good.

Women are bombarded with messages aimed specifically at them that are designed to tell or sell something—from how to look ten years younger to the best way to conquer grime in your kitchen. We are sold a bill of goods in terms of how we are supposed to appear to others. The idealized image of women on television is that of a female who is under thirty, thin, and white, and who has plenty of disposable income. Anorexic-looking young women fill the pages of fashion magazines. As a result, women of normal weight are likely to have a distorted perception of their body image. Present-day actress Courteney Cox barely tips the scales at 105 pounds, but few people know that Marilyn Monroe wore size 16 dresses!

Although advertising, the most powerful arm of the mass media, is all around us, many of us believe that we are immune to its effects. This mistaken belief is one reason advertising is so effective. The average American sees three thousand ads per day. Almost all commercial media aimed at women are supported by advertising revenue from the fashion, beauty, diet, and food industries, and their survival depends on their ability to please their sponsors through high readership levels. Magazine editors, in a fierce competition for readers, know that to make a sale, they need only play on our doubts or create new ones, making us think we have problems that don't really exist ("What's He Really Thinking When He Sees You Naked?"). Every part of the female body is picked apart and scrutinized, with most articles telling us outright which products we should buy to fix—or at least camouflage—our numerous "flaws."

The result? A depletion of our power and self-esteem. Many of us begin to objectify ourselves. When you're in an intimate moment with your partner, do you imagine what you look like from the outside rather than focus on the sensations you're feeling *inside*? When you walk down the street, are you thinking about how you appear—about how big your butt looks—instead of thinking about the beauty and life around you? Self-objectification can lead to feeling self-conscious and humiliated, and it can make us believe that our bodies exist only for the pleasure of others.

What's God Got to Do with It?

When my daughter was five years old she asked me, "Mommy, why does Daddy go to church and you don't? Don't you love God?"

"Of course I love God! Why do you ask that?"

"Because at church they teach us that if you don't go to church that means you don't love God. Are they right, Mommy?"

"No honey, they're not right, they're wrong. Your Daddy and I both believe in God, but in different ways. Neither way is right or wrong, just different. What you experience when you go to church with Daddy is what you call religion. Religion does not work for me, I live my life through spirituality."

"But how can they both be right?"

"Daddy's way is right for him because it works for him, and Mommy's way is right for her because it works for her. There is more than one way to love or worship God . . . and no one should ever tell you that their way is the only right way."

The foundation of empowerment is built on faith. I am a true believer that without faith, empowerment cannot exist. Yet I don't believe I have the right to define what faith should be for you. That's for you to decide. For myself, faith is the anchor that keeps me grounded in my power. It gives me the strength to know that no matter how bad circumstances in my life may seem, God will never give me more than I can handle. I do not believe I need religion to have a deep personal relationship with God, nor do I believe I need other individuals teaching how my relationship with God should be. It is my opinion that there is no right or wrong way to relate to God. There is only "Your Way."

Although I believe institutionalized religion can do great things for some individuals, it angers me when they each believe their religion is the true religion and everyone else's is false. I cannot make any sense of that. Every religion that dismisses any other way of worshipping God is passing judgment. Now, think about it. Would God want us to judge other people for being different?

Regardless of denomination, many people around the world spend an enormous amount of energy—and sometimes blood—trying to prove that their God is the right God and their interpretation of their holy scriptures is the right way to live. Yet would God want women, the daughters that he created, to be burned at the stake for breaking rules that deny their very existence? In a sense, burning women at the stake is not a thing of the past, it is still happening today.

Take the case of Hatun Surucu, a twenty-three-year-old Muslim Turkish immigrant woman living in Germany, who was killed by her own brother in February 2005. The reason, according to him, was that she was becoming too westernized. She had stopped wearing her head scarf, refused to go back to her family, and had declared her intent to "seek her own circle of friends." In other words, she died for trying to take back her power against her particular cultural and religious constraints.

I refuse to believe God is to be feared. I don't believe we should "fear" the being who is there to protect us. God's name has been used for centuries to perpetuate fear and shame, especially where women are concerned. With a guilt- and shame-based value system, how are we supposed to grow up to be confident women? And if God loves us, why would he want us to live that kind of life?

In the next chapter, you will find the tools needed to become a self-empowered, spiritual woman of the twenty-first century.

3 IF I HAD A HAMMER:
A TOOL KIT FOR SELF-EMPOWERMENT AND SPIRITUAL GROWTH

I was in an abusive marriage for ten years before I was able to gather the courage to walk away. Reading the book *Empowering Latinas* changed my life and gave me the tools and encouragement I needed to not let the obstacles of my past keep me from believing in myself. It helped me to get a better sense of who I am and what I'm capable of if I work hard to reach my goals. Yasmin Davidds's own story inspired me by giving me a new perspective on life. It gave me hope to follow my dreams by embracing the world instead of fearing it.

—Victoria, one of my readers and workshop participants

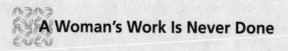 **A Woman's Work Is Never Done**

We all have one thing in common: our beliefs about ourselves—the way we see our own images and roles, the way we think we ought to be—have been directly influenced by the messages we received, and perhaps continue to receive, from our families and communities while growing up. These messages, communicated to us both verbally and nonverbally, can be either positive or negative, but they are incredibly powerful.

Because our family constituted our entire reality when we were young, we made decisions about who we were and how we were supposed to interact with others based on how our families saw the world. Many of us do not realize that much of how we feel, how we live, and what we believe has been shaped by what our parents and their parents before them believed, because that's the way it has always been.

These inherited messages, which determine most of our attitudes, judgments, and perceptions, tell us who we "should be." They define our moral values, relationships, politics, career choices, ethics, and attitudes toward education, sexuality, and finances. By subconsciously internalizing these concepts, we establish our own system of beliefs. Even if these beliefs do not make sense to our conscious mind, we will always find a way to rationalize them.

From birth, many of us have been programmed to believe everything society dictates about what is "right" for women. When a woman matures and begins to question these beliefs, she tries to change but often finds that she can't. The imposed societal beliefs have become so much a part of her that she can't seem to let go. As Christiane Northrup, M.D., author of *Women's Bodies, Women's Wisdom,* explains:

> *It is important to understand that our beliefs go much deeper than our thoughts, and we cannot simply will them away. Many beliefs are completely unconscious and are not readily available to the intellect. Most of us aren't aware of our own destructive beliefs that undermine our health. They don't come from the intellect alone, the part that thinks it's*

in control. They come from that other part that in
the past became lodged and buried in the cell tissue.

Although we *can* change, breaking free from these powerful belief systems and taking back our power is not easy. In effect, it requires creating a new belief system. First we must get in touch with what lies within our subconscious; then we must understand where it came from, how it developed, and how it has affected our lives. Through this process, we can determine which beliefs we need to eliminate in order to become more whole women. Finally, we must replace harmful, self-defeating beliefs with those that are positive and soul-enhancing.

Because our beliefs have been created mostly by what we have seen and heard, the tendency is to blame our parents. I want to emphasize, though, that our belief systems are *culturally* inherited, passed down through generations. Our parents did not create them for us. We must understand that our parents passed them down to us not because they didn't love us; doing so was simply the only way they knew *how* to love us.

Perhaps because of this ingrained cultural behavior, one of the greatest problems in many cultures is a lack of boundaries within the family structure. Boundaries give us the ability to guiltlessly grow as separate individuals; they enable us to learn that we must be loyal to ourselves before we can be loyal to others. When a cultural belief discourages taking care of ourselves first—which is the foundation of emotional well-being—it becomes a toxic belief.

It is also very important to remember that although our families have influenced us, we cannot blame them for the way our lives turn out. We must recognize any obstacles that our families may have created and take the necessary steps to get past them. We must heal the pain of the past—grieve, forgive, and move forward. Personal power is a tool for life enhancement that will gain strength when it is fueled by your belief, desire, and hope. As you build your personal power, you will find it much easier to take on new responsibilities and tackle the important choices that life presents.

The Seven Empowerment Principles

Self-empowerment is a lifelong process, twisting and bending as new challenges and situations arise. As you begin the journey to the core of your power, I must be brutally honest: it won't be easy. But few worthwhile things come without hard work. Making profound changes in your life takes a true sense of commitment and soul-searching. But by creating what I call a principle-centered life—a life made up of integrity, love, self-determination, and self-respect—you will force others to know that you mean business.

Truly empowered women live by a set of seven principles that they never deviate from. I have these written down on a piece of paper that I carry with me at all times. I suggest you do the same. These principles, which I explain in the rest of this chapter, are as follows:

1. I Own My Life
2. I Know Who I Am and What I Stand For
3. I Create Beliefs That Empower Me

4. I Live in Truth

5. I Never Feel Guilty About Being a Strong Woman

6. I Respect Myself

7. I Do First What I Fear the Most

In your quest to take back your power, you may find different feelings coming to the surface from within yourself. You may find yourself questioning many things in your life. That's fine—it's part of the process; but as you go about it, have compassion for yourself. Don't judge or blame yourself for what you did or didn't do. As I said before, you need not blame your parents, either, for things they may have done wrong. Everything they did is a result of what they knew and how they were raised. You are reading this book because you want to do better; you want to overcome. You know it is up to *you* to learn new ways to live your life and then pass those ways on to the next generation.

As you finish reading about each principle, just say to yourself, *I can do this.* Believe it as you say it, and you will get there.

Principle 1. I Own My Life

One aspect of life about which you have no choice is making choices. Life will always bring challenges, but it's not problems that determine your life—it's how you choose to respond to them that really counts. No one can do anything to you unless you give him or her permission, or unless you set yourself up to be a victim.

The only way you can change your life for the better is by taking full responsibility for everything your existence encompasses. Owning your power means owning up to the fact that you create your own circumstances, whether happy or sad, and ultimately, you are the only one who can effect real changes in your life. Your only purpose should be the purpose you name, your only destiny should be the one you create, and your only agenda should be the agenda you have decided upon for yourself. You are the writer, the director, and the star of your own production. Others can certainly participate, but you are in charge.

It's vital to remember that although you can change your life, you can't really change other people's lives and behavior. Too often, just trying is a wasted effort. Take comfort in the knowledge that you are responsible for you and only you! By taking responsibility for your success and happiness, you free yourself from emotional dependency. You become self-reliant. True freedom comes from realizing that our problems are almost always the consequences of decisions we have made. Take care not to shift blame or deny your own role in any given situation. This may seem like a difficult and abstract concept, but realize that every time you make an excuse for something, you are turning away from the truth. To live and not simply exist, you must be willing to take 100 percent responsibility for your decisions, your actions, and your words—not even 99.9 percent will do.

Personal responsibility is fundamental to living an empowered life. Without it, you will not be able to conquer the fears, frustrations, and challenges that affect you on a daily basis. As an autonomous human being, you have a responsibility to learn to be a whole person: to be emotionally and spiritually nourished, to question rules and beliefs that make no sense, and to learn all you can about your own inherent power and its uses.

Principle 2. I Know Who I Am and What I Stand For

Empowered women become successful by living life on their own terms, and the first commandment of taking control of your life is "Know Thyself." Barbara McClintock, who won the Nobel Prize in Physiology or Medicine at age eighty-one, said, "When you know you're right, you don't care what others think. You know sooner or later it will all come out in the wash." No one knows or understands you better than yourself. Each of us is our own expert, our own therapist, our own nurturer, and it only makes sense that when we are looking for understanding or direction, there is no one better, ultimately, to ask than ourselves.

There is a contradiction at work here because we do live in a culture of external expertise. We have consistently and systematically been taught that when we have a question, we should go elsewhere—whether to our parents, our church, our doctor, or our friends—for the answer, as if they know us better than we know ourselves. While it's true that other people may know specifics that can be useful to us, no one can tell us about what is happening in our bodies and minds better than we can. Seeking out knowledge or assistance from outside sources can be absolutely essential—we don't live in a vacuum—but if you are unsatisfied with your life, you must at least start the search for answers from within. Plenty of people have acquired information about any number of subjects, and anyone interested in learning should partake of their wisdom. We should never shut out what others can offer; we just need to take care that we don't take everything we hear as the gospel truth. Instead, we should draw from the well of human knowledge, integrate that knowledge the best way we can, but still retain enough self-awareness to decide how to apply it to our own lives.

There are two profound methods of knowing yourself even better. First, listen to your intuition. Trust your inner voice. Whenever you're in doubt, go with the flow of your own nature. Second, look to yourself for answers to key questions. Use external expertise as a guide, but make the final decisions yourself. Getting to know yourself is scary at first. Beyond all of the expectations and stereotypes we operate under to varying degrees, it also requires a lot of courage to be completely open and honest with ourselves. I've never met anyone who was totally satisfied with herself or who wasn't eager to explore options. Previous experience may offer valuable lessons, but too often those lessons remain undiscovered because we're reluctant to face the emotions that accompany the memories. Even if you're comfortable with deep and probing introspection, admitting mistakes and taking blame can be excruciating.

When it comes to what you choose to do with the information you pick up, how you integrate it into your life, what it means to you, and how you decide to respond to it, there is only one expert: you.

Principle 3. I Create Beliefs That Empower Me

How much do you know about yourself? Have you ever actually taken time to consider who you are apart from your work, your family, or your interests? Why do you believe the things you do about yourself? Have you ever wondered how you came to formulate your belief system?

Every belief you hold shapes your experiences. Your

thoughts create your reality. It is up to you to take control of those thoughts and consciously create a fulfilling reality. If you want to discover the reason you aren't living a life that you have chosen, ask yourself this question: What beliefs am I holding that are resulting in my feelings of dissatisfaction? If you are committed to uncovering the truth, you will peel through the layers of your unconscious mind and find the truth.

How do you stop saying, This is just the way I am, and start asking, Why am I like this? By realizing that deeply held belief systems have caused you to think the way you do. Remember that these beliefs are not of your own making; but in accepting that they are culturally inherited, don't forget to assess the role your own morals and values play in their context. It is understandable to feel some fear about changing your beliefs; you may think that doing so will destroy the essence of who everyone else thinks you are. But if you really think about it, does what you blindly believe right now truly reflect who *you* are?

Principle 4. I Live in Truth

By finding your personal truth and creating your life around it, you will find serenity. Living your truth is finding the essence of yourself, validating it fully, and welcoming it into full expression. An empowered woman is a woman who has made a real effort to find her truth and then relies on it consistently. She bases her life on authenticity.

When we were young children, we lived authentically, seldom afraid or embarrassed to seek out what we wanted or to speak our minds. Now that we've grown up, we tend to tuck away the "real us" in our attempts to fit in, to please, to be noticed, to be loved . . . the list goes on and on. But subconsciously, we never entirely let go of that desire to express ourselves freely. We may conform to society's mores while privately embracing secret passions, but hiding those desires doesn't change the fact that we possess them. It is important never to stray too far from that boldness and self-interest of childhood—it is a quality that can only help you, as long as you don't go overboard.

The simplest way to live your truth is to leave behind the expectations of others and live the way you choose; don't make decisions based on what your family or the media or the church say. When you're living your truth, you cannot be dissuaded from following your heart. It means being selfish in a healthy way by doing what you know is best for you, regardless of the opinions of others—even close friends and family. Living authentically means that you make choices without fear, trusting in the wisdom of your soul.

In an ideal world, we should all have careers that make us happy; we should decide whether we want to marry and have children; we should wear what we want, say what we want, and like what we want without fear that we'll be uncool, undutiful, or shameful. Of course, we don't live in an ideal world, and we all know that compromise and understanding are what make us civilized. However, there is a middle ground between compromise and understanding and your trust in your beliefs, where you'll never be afraid to speak your truth and live by it. Because you trust yourself so much, there won't be a person on earth who will be able to make better decisions for you than yourself.

In living your truth, there are no pretenses. Everything you do will reflect self-esteem and self-awareness. Denying your unique truth only leads to feelings of failure and dissatisfaction because you are essentially ignoring yourself. Honor your strengths instead. Actively seek them out. Discover what pleases you, whether it's fashion, physics, bodybuilding, or politics. Don't rely on other people, including those on television and in magazines, for opinions. Discover your passions by trying new things, then stick with the ones that stir your soul. Finding who you really are and then making the choice to embrace that person takes time and work. With each new truth you acknowledge about yourself, with each new action you take that reflects what you really like, you find an inner peace that lets you know you're on the right track. Living in truth is the foundation for all other life work.

Principle 5. I Never Feel Guilty About Being a Strong Woman

The only way to win the game of guilt is not to play. Don't ever apologize for who you are, and don't ever feel ashamed about your power.

"Loyalty before all—or else" is a common belief in many families and cultures. As children, we are taught that devotion to our family and their beliefs supersedes all, without question. But decisions made solely out of loyalty, with no consideration for practicality or ethics, can be dangerous. In too many situations, when we try to show some independence, we are made to feel guilty. Because we don't know better, we engage in the guilt game, hoping and yearning that sooner or later "they" will understand us and change. We continue to seek approval by abiding by unrealistic demands, and then we are disappointed in ourselves for doing so. This constant struggle drains our energy, leaving us with no hope of being satisfied.

I've been approached by so many women who want help "changing" their mothers, husbands, sisters, daughters, and other people in their lives. I always tell these women, "You cannot control whether or not anyone changes, they can only change if *they* choose to change. The only person you can change is yourself. You can't depend on anyone to change in order for *you* to be free. You need to believe that we are all entitled to be our real, authentic selves—you, too!"

When you have reached the point where you are totally connected to your own inner power, your intuition, and your truth, it won't even occur to you to be ashamed of or apologize for what you've become. You made the decision to change. Others will react. But because that connection brings you so much confidence and self-awareness, others will begin to see that your newfound power is a blessing. It only enhances who you are. The affirmations in Chapter Eight, "Follow the Yellow Brick Road," will help you to see that you teach others how to treat you; you show them that, as much as they matter, you matter, too.

Principle 6. I Respect Myself

Your body is a temple, and your soul is where your higher power—or your intuition—lives. Both need nourishment. So many of us are dissociated from ourselves, in particular our bodies. We expect so much from the form we've been given, yet we pay it so little respect. Our minds work all day solving problems and making plans, yet we rarely take time to be thankful for the power of intellect. Our souls communicate hugely important messages to us—they guide and protect us—yet we regularly neglect to celebrate our soul inspiration.

Self-respect is about honoring every part of you, by whatever means necessary. When your body is tired, you must allow it to rest. It's no surprise that most of us treat our homes and cars much better than we treat our physical beings; we're busy, and we've been distracted from focusing on ourselves. It requires action on your part to make things right between you and your physicality. It takes the development of a healthy self-respect, which means facing your fear of shame. Luckily, building that self-respect will help you face all of your fears.

Self-respect also means being thankful. When you love yourself, you can delight in your ability to speak for yourself, to have your own opinions, to make your own lifestyle choices. Being able to manifest your energy in such a positive way is something to celebrate. Self-respect absolutely includes celebrating who you are and giving yourself credit. When you love yourself and know yourself, it seems like the most natural thing in the world.

People will treat you only the way you allow yourself to be treated. If you want others to respect you, begin by respecting yourself. That means standing up for yourself and not allowing anyone to mistreat you in any way. Learning self-respect is a long process, but with each step you take in the right direction, you contribute to your own well-being.

Principle 7. I Do First What I Fear the Most

Almost all of our decisions stem from either fear or love. One example: we go to work either because we love our work or because we fear that if we don't show up, we'll get fired! Realize, though, that making decisions from a place of fear will always weaken you; also keep in mind that 90 percent of what we fear never actually comes to pass.

Sometimes fear can protect you, but that's no excuse for letting it stifle you. Allowing life to bless you often boils down to not fighting fear and pain. You can numb yourself to pain, but a void is exactly what it sounds like—nothing. In doing so, you run the great risk of cutting yourself off from happiness, too. The essence of life is feeling, and we cannot turn our backs on one emotion without losing the others.

The key to facing your fears is remembering that problems are gifts wrapped with altogether too much tape. When we accept the gift and cut through all of the tape, the fear disappears. Challenges invite us to learn, and once we've acknowledged the unknown and seen that it isn't as bad as we thought, the problem disappears. Fear can be the most limiting emotion a woman can have. It leads to missed opportunities, worry, and a slow suffocation of the soul.

This is terribly important: If you have tried everything to face your fears (including the exercises in Chapter Eight) and are still struggling, there is one method I have always relied on: ask your higher power—whether God or a power you call by another name—for help. Simply say, *I can't do this by myself. I open my mind and heart and ask you to carry me through this situation. Do through me whatever needs to be done.*

Your Journey Toward a New Spiritual Self

To introduce you to the process of spiritual self-discovery, I've compiled a list of ten aspects of that endeavor. It is your journey and, therefore, your decision whether to consider a new way of thinking.

1. Awareness

You must understand and accept that there is a strong powerful force (your higher power) that will guide you through tragedies and lead you to joy, whether you are Christian, Jewish, Hindu, Buddhist, or Islamic. What you call your higher power is up to you, so long as it is an empowering force that never inspires fear. What matters most is that this higher power allows you to feel safe, secure, and powerful. Remember, in spirituality there is no such thing as an angry or spiteful God. Your higher power is all-loving, nonjudgmental, and serene.

2. Willingness

You must be willing to open your heart to whatever comes your way, whether it is joy, pain, frustration, love, fear, or anger. Before we can truly feel our emotions, we must have enough faith to let our guard down. Some of us find it nearly impossible to risk giving in to emotion. If you can develop a healthy spirituality, it will provide you with your anchor—it will ease your fear and help you understand why you are afraid. Even better, this sense of spirituality makes it easier to find serenity and bliss. Allow yourself to do three things that give you peace every day.

When you can define your *own* peace for yourself, you are living from your soul.

3. Intuition

Trust your intuition; it's the voice of your higher power. Use your intuition as a source, as a guide. If something *feels* wrong, your gut feelings are almost always correct and you can thank your intuition for taking good care of you; the key is that *you* are taking care of *you*. This mysterious force of intuition is sacred. It may come to you in many different forms, because it is literally a force that flows through you, given to you at birth by your higher power. Don't be afraid to explore new areas and interests because of possible judgment from others. If your intuition tells you to try meditation or take up writing or art—go for it!

4. Acceptance

Give yourself permission to explore your true feelings about religion, God, and spirituality. Ask yourself the following questions:

• Do your religious or spiritual beliefs come from within your soul, or are they just something you learned and never questioned?

• Do these beliefs encourage you to be who you truly want to be, or do they hold you back?

• If your beliefs hold you back from living the life you want to live, have you ever questioned the source of those beliefs?

It will take time to find real answers to these questions. Be patient. Once you have begun to form your ideas about religion and spirituality, make sure you own them. Don't let judgment or guilt or family concerns sway you from what you truly believe and how you choose to live your life with your God. Accept your faith and respect yourself for recognizing your real inner power—the one you were born with.

5. Truth

It's amazing that something so simple should be so complicated. Living in truth is the easiest, calmest, happiest way you can choose to live. Everyone knows what living in truth means—we're just too scared to admit it because we feel shame about the lies we're living. You know what your truth is. You know what you think is right and what isn't. And it doesn't make a bit of difference what anyone else thinks. You can share your truth with others, as I do, or you can take comfort in knowing that you are honest with yourself and above reproach. You are not judged, and you will not be judged, because judgment means nothing to you, especially when it comes from people who are clawing their way through their own web of lies. You need to recognize the difference between what you were told is the truth and what your mind and body tell you is the truth.

6. Choices

Choose to include people in your life who honor you and your spiritual process. Friends and family who project negativity only frustrate your self-discovery. Can aspects of your life be creatively reorganized so that you can spend more time with positive people who are doing positive things? The first steps are always the most difficult, but investigating your choices will make them more familiar. You have the power to change any negative aspect of your life. You do not need money, a better opportunity, or luck. It is your willingness and commitment to live a better life that makes change possible.

7. Love

Be open to receiving love, especially from yourself. Understand that your higher power, expressed through your intuition, will never cause you to feel stressed, pressured, or full of doubt. Those emotions come from not believing in yourself and not trusting that higher power. Your higher power will only bring you love, awareness, energy, and joy. Allow yourself to be who you truly are; if you do not know who you are yet, be who you've always wanted to be. The important thing is to avoid being what others want you to be. I find it amazing that so many women think they gain love by pleasing others. Find activities that make you feel proud, and then partake in those activities as often as possible.

8. Immediacy

Think of today as the first day of the rest of your life, and live as though it were your last. If you have made mistakes, learn from them, and then vow never to make them again. In the end, your past is just that, dust in the wind. But it will repeat itself if you don't make adjustments. If you are always living on a "schedule" (which I am guilty of), make room for an activity that's spontaneous and new.

9. Fearlessness

Women have been taught to fear the outside world, and this has limited our ability to fulfill our destinies. The world is full of marvelous possibilities, which too often go unrealized because of fear. What are your greatest fears? Why do you fear them? Do you know where your fear comes from? When you think about it, most of our fears stem from tradition and a sense of impending failure that society has instilled in us. Your intuition is your most trusted and valuable tool, and when used, it can make the world your oyster.

10. Faith

It is often difficult to know when you have found faith because it is such an abstract concept. If you begin to second-guess yourself, it can be very frustrating. The solution is to form an unshakable and complete confidence in yourself and allow your higher power to fill you up with strength when you're feeling weak. When you believe in yourself, anything is possible. Your higher power is that confidence, and your faith is what makes it so strong. When you access your higher power's strength, you are unstoppable.

We'll be exploring these steps in more depth in Chapter Eight, the exercises section of this book.

4
MAY
THE POWER
BE WITH
YOU

I tried being myself once, but it didn't work. I realized
I didn't have enough experience.
—A seminar participant

I've found that the more failures I experience, the
more I learn—and learning what *doesn't* work for you is
every bit as important as learning what *does* work for you.
At one point in my career, I felt a deep need to search for
answers as to which direction I wanted to take. I read
dozens of books, sought advice from friends and professionals, and even hired a business coach to provide me with
these elusive answers. I looked for signs from the outside
world; I asked God to give me direction. But the more I
searched *outside* myself, the more distressed I became. All
of the books I read said the same thing: "You need to look
within yourself, because you already have all of the answers." Frankly, I thought it was one of the stupidest things
I'd ever heard.

I thought, How can I have the answers inside of me if
I don't know anything about this business, if I don't have

the necessary expertise? Looking within for answers seemed virtually impossible. How could I trust myself when I didn't even know what I was doing? Then it hit me: it was all about *trust*. It was about trusting that insistent inner voice—the one that speaks from the heart and soul, not the mind—to tell me to do what was right.

It's important to distinguish between those two voices we all carry, because sometimes our intellectual voice simply doesn't have the same instinctual knowledge as the inner-core voice. Your soul will never give you the same plan of action as your mind, but it will give you the *truth*—not your parents' truth, or your boss's truth, but *your* truth. If you can learn to really listen, as Luz does in the following story, your soul will give you the answer.

 Luz's Story: Never Too Late

Luz was a precocious little girl, full of hopes and dreams, showered with affection by her mother and father. At just five years old, an age when most children are occupied with dolls and toys, she declared to anyone who would listen, "One day I'm going to be the president of my very own big company. I'm just like my daddy. I have the will."

For her tenth birthday, Luz received many gifts, but the one that caught her attention was a Sno-Kone machine. Right away, she set it up on the sidewalk in front of her house, cranked it up, and began selling tamarind-flavored ice cones for a dime. As neighbors stopped by to buy her cool confections, her piggy bank began to fill, and Luz's business dreams and self-confidence took off. She had become an entrepreneur and truly believed she could accomplish anything she set her mind to.

Then, when she was twelve years old, Luz's body began to develop. Unlike her friends, Luz was embarrassed by the attention her new curves attracted. She had always shied away from boys, while her girlfriends seemed completely obsessed with them. Luz noticed that the other girls didn't daydream about their own exciting careers. Instead they would say, "Boys don't like girls who are too smart." Day after day she watched the girls fawn over the boys, giggling, batting their eyelashes, and acting as if they didn't have a thought in their heads. Luz refused to play this game and began to keep to herself. She lost most of her friends, and the boys made fun of her when she participated in class, calling her a "kiss-up" and "teacher's pet." Luz had been very good at sports, but with her changing body, and the changing attitudes around her, she no longer participated. It just wasn't fun anymore.

Acting dumb and demure to attract a boy seemed ridiculous to Luz, but like all girls her age, she wanted desperately to belong. Little by little, and feeling unnatural about it, she began to compromise herself. She read glamour magazines and bought new, tight-fitting, sexy clothes that, although they felt very uncomfortable at first, made her believe that she could blend into the crowd—maybe even be noticed. Luz managed to stifle her independent spirit, and by the time she reached high school, she was speaking less and disguising her true self more. She let the boys think they had all the right answers, even when she knew full well they were wrong. Luz was no longer the outspoken, energetic, inventive, and confident little business girl selling Sno-Kones on the sidewalk. Now she was focused on pleasing the people around her.

After high school, Luz went on to college and studied business. She was on the right track, but the damage had already been done. The messages she'd taken to heart as a teenager would be hard to erase. When she was dating Thomas, her fiancé, Luz kept quiet about her aspirations, fearing that her ambition would scare him away. She thought perhaps she'd tell him when their relationship was more secure. Graduation came and went, and she was too busy planning their wedding and making a home to consider burdening her new husband with her own goals.

Shortly after their wedding, Luz became pregnant. Before the baby was born, she finally found the courage to tell Thomas that she wanted to start an employment agency to assist women who have been out of the workplace for some time. She explained that with his help, she could handle both the baby and the company. To her disappointment, Thomas left no room for any discussion whatsoever. He had strong opinions and insisted that Luz stay home until the child began school. They argued back and forth for several weeks, until Luz, not wanting to jeopardize their marriage, put her dreams on hold—again.

When their son was three, Thomas told Luz he wanted a sibling for his little boy to play with. Luz explained that since Carlitos was almost in preschool, this would be the perfect time for her to set up her business. Thomas again dismissed her plan. A few days later, at a family gathering, he announced to everyone that they were planning to have another child. Naturally, everyone congratulated Luz for being such a dedicated wife and mother. Again she gave in.

Once her second child reached school age, Luz finally had some time for herself. She began reading about powerful women and tried to envision herself as one, but in her mind's eye, she saw a much younger woman. Is it too late for me? Have I wasted the best years of my life? she asked herself. Although both of her children were in school, Luz was still exhausted at night after managing the household all day and seeing to the needs of the kids and Thomas when they came home. Luz was on the verge of giving up her dreams entirely. One morning, she found herself driving through her old neighborhood, and she pulled up to the house where she'd grown up. She got out of the car and walked over to the spot where her old Sno-Kone stand had once stood, and she began to cry as memories of her childhood dreams washed over her. God, why did you let me give up my dream in order to please a man? Now I have no energy to start my life over!

She heard a voice inside her head: "You already have the gift of power, will, and strength to fulfill your dreams. It was your choice to misuse those gifts. At birth, you were given unlimited power to live a full life, not to give it away to others. Reclaim this power, and you will find renewed strength to pursue any dream." For more than an hour, Luz sat on the curb, digesting what had just happened. The message was loud and clear: to bring back the happiness and confidence she'd once had as a child, she needed to rediscover the spirit of that child.

Just as important, she knew she had to take control of her own decisions and share her revelations with her own doubting Thomas. She prayed for his support, but Luz had made up her mind to follow her own path, even without his support. Thomas was shocked at first, but he listened carefully. Finally, after years of their being together, he recognized the strength of the woman who stood in front of him. Luz was thrilled when Thomas admitted that he couldn't help being impressed by her conviction.

Ready to begin making her dreams a reality, Luz created a plan. She drew up a list of all the people and things that had influenced her and her decisions as far back as she could remember, including her parents, her children, and her friends. Then she made a commitment to ask each of them for their help and support in reaching her goals, both business and personal. Luz listed her daily duties next—tasks such as housework and grocery shopping. It was a long list. Finding it difficult to ignore, disrespect, or argue with Luz's new persona, Thomas agreed to any necessary changes. They reached an agreement: Thomas would take on half of the family and household responsibilities until Luz's business turned a profit, and then they would hire someone to help.

With this agreement in place, Luz finally put her brain and education to use and opened the business she'd dreamed of her whole life. She was blossoming, radiant, and happier than she'd ever been. Thomas, on the other hand, missed his old lifestyle. He longed for the days when Luz was waiting for him to come home from work, with dinner on the table. He missed relaxing in front of the TV with his wife there at his beck and call. It wasn't long before he vocalized his frustrations and begged Luz to give up the business for a "normal" family life again.

Luz could easily have given in. So many women are eventually forced or persuaded to give up their power, even if they've been fortunate enough to taste it for themselves. But Luz believed *enough*. She had rediscovered her personal power, and she wasn't going to let it go.

One night, after a long talk, Luz told Thomas something he finally understood. "I'm not asking you to give up your life for me, like I did for you," she said. "All I'm asking for is my fair share. You have your own personal life and career, and I want mine, too. I deserve it."

When Luz found a way to tap into her inner strength, she learned to stand up for herself and make it known that she would not take no for an answer, not even from her husband. Thomas realized in the end that Luz's opinions really were worth listening to.

It's all in the approach. When we realize the magnitude of our own power, we can achieve anything, and we can do it with confidence, grace, and peace of mind. We need not alienate or attack; we simply need to know what's best for us and communicate it clearly and honestly to those whom we need to persuade to our side.

What "Owning Your Power" Means

Each of us has power over our own lives, but many of us misunderstand this power and don't fully utilize it. We let other people make decisions for us, or we base our decisions on *their* expectations. As a result, some of us are leading very unhappy lives. A woman who recognizes her true potential draws on her *personal power,* and uses that power to make decisions for herself in every aspect of her life.

Personal power comes from within. Once you embrace it, you know that there is nothing in the world you can't handle. It helps you recognize that everything in your life is a choice, and it reinforces the truth that you have complete control over every choice you make. Personal power is directly related to the love we have for ourselves; it is not driven by ego or material possessions. The more we learn to love ourselves, the more power we have to shape our own futures without being manipulated by others.

Although we may not have control over all events in our lives, we *do* have control over how we react to those events. Negativity is insidious, and it affects our peace of mind every day if we let it. Negative people can cause us to make harmful choices, and we all know how hard it is to avoid certain people's influence, for any number of reasons. The beauty of personal power is that it helps to deflect negative energy. It will help you maintain the perspective you need to do what's right according to you and you alone.

Personal power motivates you to seek happiness rather than remain in and complain about unpleasant situations. If the traditions that have shaped your life are stifling you, then you must draw on your personal power for inspiration so that you can create your own guidelines without guilt or worry about offending others. How do you create your own guidelines? The first step is to trust yourself enough to own your power. I know the concept seems abstract, but what it really means is feeling safe and secure with the decisions you make. The truth is, you can count on yourself above anyone else.

- Owning your power means loving yourself.
- Owning your power means feeling comfortable with your power.

• Owning your power means arriving at a wanted destination in life and still remaining whole as a person.

• Owning your power means never trading away your unique characteristics or what you enjoy to please anyone else.

• Owning your power means staying in your own center of truth all of the time.

Whose Life Is It, Anyway?

The key to self-empowerment is the ability to make good choices. Yet most women have been conditioned to put everyone else's needs above their own. They have been taught to take a *passive* approach to life. They have allowed themselves to believe that it's a man's job to take care of them. As a result, women have automatically and subconsciously handed over their personal power and decision-making rights to the men in their lives. This passivity creates feelings of inadequacy in many women and leaves them unable to make *any* healthy decisions on their own. Time after time, women of diverse ethnicities have told me that they don't think they're smart or strong enough to control their own lives. It's critical to remember that when we don't exercise our personal power, we become vulnerable to circumstances as well as to other people.

On the other hand, someone who is *proactive* will draw on her personal power to help her make all of her own choices, whether she's deciding something as simple as where to go for dinner or as significant as whether to launch a new career. A proactive woman aggressively pursues alternatives instead of handing over her life on a silver platter . . . and with zipped lips.

Every decision you make affects your well-being. It's never too late to take control, to begin developing and exercising your decision-making skills, and to adopt proactive attitudes. Behaving passively, complying with your partner's every wish, putting your wants and needs on hold, or changing your demeanor to suit someone else's idea of what's right or pretty or cool is unacceptable.

Five Steps to Freedom and Personal Power

Taking her power back from a controlling person or situation can be one of the most courageous acts of a woman's life. Although at first you may think that breaking free is impossible, I promise that it's worth it. The famous quote by President Franklin Delano Roosevelt is absolutely correct: "The only thing we have to fear is fear itself." The rewards of personal freedom are monumental, and you can't revel in them until you've broken through the various chains that are binding you to a passive life.

Freedom and personal power go hand in hand. Freedom means living your life as you choose, demonstrating power over your own actions. In order to begin the process of empowerment, you must believe this—and follow these five steps:

Step 1. Awareness
You must become aware of who and what hold the most power over you. What kind of power do they have

over you? How do they hold this power over you? Why do they have power over you? When do they exert this power over you?

Step 2. Understanding

You need to understand *why* you allow others to have power over you. Remember: no one can take your power unless you give it to that person. There is usually some kind of reward that comes with giving your power away. Does being under someone else's control make you feel safe and secure? Do you allow it so that he or she won't get angry? Do you give your power away to feed someone else's ego? Do you just want people to like you? It is very important that you find the answers to these questions so that this "reward" can be replaced with healthier patterns of behavior. Identifying the benefit you receive by allowing another person to control your life is key to the process of self-empowerment.

Step 3. Desire to Change

Unless you have a real and true desire to take back your personal power, it simply won't happen, because the minute you receive resistance from your controllers, you'll probably give in. Your passion for change is what keeps you moving forward.

Step 4. Planning

Create a *strategic empowerment plan* that details how you will take back control of your life. This type of plan helps you determine exactly which goals—such as becoming more assertive, getting an education, or telling a family member no—you want to achieve. Your plan should also include strategies for reaching your empowerment goals, a time frame for achieving them, and how you will proceed once you've reached them. A sample plan can be found in Chapter Eight.

Step 5. Implementation

Once you have devised your unique strategic plan, you must love yourself enough to put it into action. As you begin to take back your personal power, you will immediately feel more in control of your life. Eventually your strategic plan will cease being a "plan" because it will have become your life.

These five steps may seem simple, but they require introspection, discipline, and hard work. Nothing worthwhile comes easy. There are myriad other steps you can take to reclaim your power, but they must make sense to *you,* and they must be steps that fulfill your dreams, not your family's or your friends' dreams for you. You have had a vision of your adult life ever since you were a little girl; you mustn't compromise that vision for any reason. When a strong woman puts her mind, heart, and will into something, she can achieve whatever she desires (no matter what you've heard in the past). It's your job to nurture yourself, to ask yourself questions that will help you sort out the mixed messages you've received over the years, and to stand up for yourself. It's up to you to make decisions that enhance your personal power and freedom, whether they involve breaking up a relationship, quitting a job, or telling your sister that you cannot watch her children day after day. It's your responsibility to learn what is best for you and to act upon that knowledge.

The Not-So-Secret Formula

During my sophomore year of college, I finally asked my mother why she'd stayed with an abusive and unfaithful husband for so long. "I couldn't leave him because he was all I had," she replied.

"What about you? You had yourself!" I said in a mild outburst of indignation.

"I honestly believed your father would take care of me forever, so I thought I didn't need an education. I wanted to leave him, but if I did, how would I have been able to provide the good life I wanted for you and your sisters? I was forced to stay in an unhappy marriage because he paid the bills. Whatever you do, *mi hijita,* remember that a man is not your salvation. Your education is your salvation!"

From that day on, my mother's heart-wrenching admission renewed my drive to study hard and finish my studies. I thought that no woman should have to make that kind of sacrifice so that her daughters wouldn't have to.

The formula to avoid being trapped in this dilemma consists of six obvious steps:

1. Get an Education
As my mother's story shows, education is the single most important tool for women who want to live independent, successful, and fulfilling lives. Not only does a formal degree lead to a higher-paying, more prestigious

(and therefore more satisfying) job, but the act of learning itself also helps us to strengthen our emotions and prepare for life's challenges. It makes us feel better about ourselves when we complete an assignment or finish reading a book, or if we meet a fascinating person or learn something new. It is so very important to realize that you don't have to be in your teens, or even in your twenties or thirties, to pursue a higher education. Universities, community and city colleges, and extension programs are open to everyone, regardless of age. Whether you are pursuing a degree, simply learning about something that interests you, or improving your chances for a promotion, enrolling in classes can open up a whole new world. Most important, doing so is guaranteed to raise your self-esteem.

2. Invest in Yourself for the Long Run

One of the main reasons many women put off their education is short-term gratification. Making decisions based on immediate results is a common deterrent to accomplishing long-term goals. Instead of looking ahead toward fulfilling an objective, we choose the instant reward, even if it doesn't seem like a reward at the time. If you choose to work full-time after high school rather than continuing your education, the paycheck is the short-term lure. Unfortunately, you are also capping your value in the marketplace because it's unlikely that your salary will rise much over the years, regardless of how hard you work. Saving for retirement, saving for your children's education, even buying a home or a car will be extremely difficult without a degree or at least technical training.

There's no getting around it—you must incorporate patience into your personality if you are going to plan your life around long-term gratification, which is geared toward accomplishing goals for a better quality of life. Continuing your education directly after high school may leave you without extra money for the movies, but in ten years you may well own a movie theater. With long-term gratification, your choices are limitless.

In order for people to make choices, they must believe they have alternatives. It is up to us to create those alternatives so that we never feel stuck. Even when we make bad decisions, we carry something valuable away from the experience. When you draw on your personal power to make your own decisions, you let go of the past and look with hope toward the future. If school is not an appropriate choice for you, there are other routes to success. As your love for yourself grows, you will find it easier to find your path, you will more easily recognize what makes you happy, and you will make the right choices for yourself.

3. Take Personal Responsibility

In ancient times, the concept of personal responsibility did not exist, and with good reason. Our ancestors did not have the choice to live "emotionally healthy" lives. Survival was the primary goal, and every action was a group responsibility toward reaching that objective. In the wild, people work together, pooling their strength to better their chances of staying alive. But as much as some men might like to preserve cave culture, times have changed. Now we must embrace our individuality and learn to distinguish our own boundaries from those of others, especially our family.

I am frequently asked questions about boundaries. One common question is, Can I set limits and be a loving person at the same time? The answer is yes. In fact, if you take the time to nurture and care for yourself—if you love yourself and are a happy person—you will spend less time worrying and feeling bad. You'll have more to offer because you'll *be* more.

Another question I often hear: What if my husband or my friends get upset or hurt by my new boundaries? Sometimes our families and friends confuse setting boundaries with being selfish. Our familial relationships are so emotionally important to us that at times we passively comply and ignore our own needs. If we don't set boundaries, emotional chaos can literally ruin our lives. We must be able to differentiate between selfishness and individuality—and what's more, we have to be able to talk confidently with our families about those differences. Be warned: people will test your limits in order to see how serious you are. Once you have set your boundaries, you must abide by them. Adhering to newly established stances is difficult, particularly for women who hold on to feelings of guilt and shame. We'll work on releasing those worthless feelings through exercises in Chapter Eight.

Isolation is another common fear. If we set boundaries, will we be separated from the people we love? We all know women who stay in harmful relationships out of fear of being alone. To combat this fear, we must expose truth; we must open up to people who will support us instead of tearing us down. We need information and empathy in order to overcome the negative images embedded in our minds by a culture that has a tendency not to respect our boundaries.

This is a time when we really need one another, girl-friends. Creating new boundaries can be scary, and it's essential to have a support system. There will be times when our sense of guilt will supersede what is right for us, and we all need someone we can call on for courage, understanding, and moral support. You are never alone in your journey; there are millions of women around the world who are struggling with the very same issues that you are.

Learning to set your own boundaries may take some time. We have no control over what others think; nor can we control their reactions to our own newly developed set of boundaries. We have only our personal responsibility to stand upon—and that's enough! Everyone deserves an explanation; it's perfectly legitimate for you to sit down and tell your family members (together or individually) that you have decided to grow up and behave like a woman. You can explain to friends and family that you have made the choice to own your personal power, and you hope they will respect your decision. If you run into a brick wall, if the reaction is negative and there are people who refuse to respect your boundaries, you may wish to limit your interaction with them. You are that important. Your responsibility to yourself must come first—that is the definition of personal responsibility.

4. Learn to Say No

"No" is a short word in just about any language, yet it may be the most powerful word a young girl ever learns. "No, I don't want to play doctor," "No, I don't want to get in the car with you," and "No, I don't want you to touch me there" are all statements that we hope all little girls would say in certain situations. Unfortunately, many of us have forgotten how to use the word.

When we teach our children to speak out and say no when they feel threatened, they learn to protect and stand up for themselves. As adults, they will feel comfortable saying "No, I will not be disrespected," "No, I do not agree with you," and the most important no they can utter: "No, I will not be a victim."

5. Tap into Your Strengths

By definition, "courage" is doing what you feel is right despite fear, anxiety, worry, doubt, and indecision. Courage is inside everyone, and although it's an admirable characteristic, for women it's a bit more complicated. In many cultures, a woman who takes a courageous stand to live her life as she chooses is seen as disrespectful and even blasphemous. Courage is supposed to be evident only in men.

Think about it: we come from a long line of courageous women, women who have lived through terrible tragedies and pain. So what is it that holds us back from exercising our courage in order to live more fulfilling lives, now that we live in a conducive environment? Fear. Fear of abandonment, fear of not being loved, and fear of being thought of as selfish or disrespectful; these are the core feelings that keep us bound. We are afraid to be judged as bad mothers, daughters, wives, or employees, so we tolerate a way of life that hurts us. We hold on to our husbands and adult children because we don't know what we'll feel if we let go.

Dedicating time and energy to *ourselves* is something many women are unfamiliar or uncomfortable with. Therefore, the three most difficult challenges we face are

• Truly believing that it is okay—that it is correct—for us to love ourselves.

- Healing our fears by re-creating a belief system that honors us. This means discovering the subconscious beliefs that do not work for us anymore, and then replacing them with a new set of beliefs that do.
- Letting go of responsibilities that don't belong to us.

Women tend to take on everyone else's problems as their own, but unless we let go of trying to fix other people's problems, we can never truly be free. Yes, it is good and compassionate to be there for family and friends, to help someone through a problem or tough time, but it is another thing to worry, stew, cry, and make yourself sick trying to solve problems, entanglements, and dramas that aren't yours. On this point, we could take a cue from men. Unless we allow the people we love to work through their own issues, they will not learn their own lessons. In every problem, there is a lesson to be learned; let it be *their* lesson.

6. Be Yourself

Making the choice to become who you really are—who you were meant to be—is the first step. Making a commitment to stick to the process is equally important. If you can find enough love in your heart for yourself to accept the power you were born with, you can experience miracles. If I had to sum up the secret formula to taking back your power in one sentence, it would be:

YOU MUST HAVE THE WILLINGNESS TO DO WHATEVER IT TAKES.

It sounds easy, but we all know how complicated life change is. Having the willingness to do whatever it takes means never giving up the quest for what you want (within ethical limits, of course). Doing whatever it takes means that even if your husband leaves you, you lose your job, your best friend turns her back on you, or you lose everything you have, you will refuse to give up or give in. Being sidetracked, procrastinating, or even taking a break is part of the process, but doing whatever it takes to tap in to your power is mental—it is an attitude of commitment.

Once you realize that you actually do deserve a better life and you make a commitment to change, certain clichés—"When God closes a door, he opens a window," "Every cloud has a silver lining"—begin to ring true. When the energy you project is positive and forward moving, you will attract people and circumstances that facilitate your journey. You will find people who will encourage you, and you will notice cues and signs along the way that confirm that what you are doing is right.

Let's say you have made the commitment to break free from an abusive relationship. For the first time, you will be acutely aware of people who can help you, whether a support group that advertises in your local paper or a woman you meet at the grocery store who is going through the same experience. It's not as if these potential support resources didn't exist before; it's just that you never focused on them—our brains can be very selective. Once you commit yourself to the process, though, you can't help visualizing success. What would it be like to achieve self-love and personal power? How would your life be affected?

In her book *The Courage to Be Yourself,* Sue Patton Thoele suggests taping a three-by-five-inch index card on your refrigerator or mirror or in your wallet that reads, "Nobody said it would be easy!" Too often we face seemingly impossible challenges and we shy away because we think that being faced with such obstacles means we're somehow bad or weak, or the world is against us. That is the attitude of a victim, my friends. Even more devastating, if we accept this victim mentality, we never discover how strong and creative we really are. Change isn't easy, but if we avoid the difficulties in our lives, we'll never conquer fear. When we face challenges and win, or when we overcome fears or don't let someone disrespect us, we experience the thrill of personal power.

The greatest rewards in life come from taking risks, from taking on the challenge of being the best possible person you can be. You do this for yourself first and then for the rest of the world. You already have the courage inside; you just need to learn to connect with it and then trust it.

5
KILLING ME SOFTLY:
SEX AS A WEAPON OF MASS OBSTRUCTION

When I'm good I'm very, very good; but when I'm bad, I'm better.
—Mae West, American actress of the 1930s

Women everywhere are expected, and sometimes even forced, to be "good" in order to be loved and accepted. In Latino culture, for example, we are supposed to live by the "Buena Rules" throughout our lives: *Buena hija. Buena esposa. Buena madre.* A good daughter, a good wife, a good mother. But a new generation of empowered females are responding with a loud "Booorrring!" to the confines of such rigid roles. No doubt, we girls do wanna have fun, but do we know how? When it comes to fun in bed, it seems no one is really laughing.

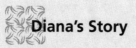 **Diana's Story**

After a fifteen-year marriage, Diana went through a divorce. With hopes of starting anew, she lost twenty pounds and set her mind to going out and enjoying herself.

She felt that she had finally become liberated, that she was in control, and that she had a whole new perspective on life, men, and sex. Believing that she was very much sexually aware, Diana made a decision: she would feel free to have casual sex. It would be fun, and she had to admit that she felt great when a man found her attractive. If men could have casual sex with no commitment, then why couldn't she?

It made her feel powerful—at first. One night at a bar, Diana met Mark. She thought he was the total package: handsome and sweet, but strong. They talked for hours over drinks, laughing at each other's jokes. His flirtation intensified, and Diana knew she could "have" him that night, but she thought twice and decided to wait until their second date. The next night, the two met for dinner and drinks, and before long they were in bed at her place. Diana was thrilled—she felt a real connection to Mark, and she enjoyed their sexual encounter. Feeling very pleased with herself, she fell asleep, only to be awakened at three in the morning as Mark attempted to sneak out, mumbling something about having to work early. He promised he would call.

Three days later, he had not called. Diana was bothered, though she didn't want to admit it. After all, she was playing by the boys' rules now. She fought the urge to allow her emotions to take over. On day five, she answered the phone to a cheerful and relaxed Mark telling her what a wonderful time he'd had with her. She couldn't help feeling elated when he suggested meeting again, though he wouldn't be available for a week or so. Diana hung up the phone, unable to deny her feelings. She was relieved and giddy, even though Mark's schedule seemed odd. Two weeks later he called again, they met for dinner, and once again they ended up between the sheets. As had happened before, very early in the morning, Mark left, promising to call her in a few weeks so they could "hook up" again. This time, Diana just offered a weak smile, and as soon as he left, she began to cry, thinking to herself, What the hell is wrong with me? Why am I so sad?

As emotions often do, hers had finally taken over. The fact is, Diana felt used—because she *was* being used. Her original intent had been to join the ranks of the "users"— not to get emotionally involved. Mark had succeeded in distancing himself, but she had failed, and therein lies the difference between men and women: men can enjoy a sexual relationship on a purely physical basis, without an iota of shame, guilt, or emotional investment, but most women can't. Some women may want to believe that they can separate their emotions from their sexuality, but ultimately they are left with emptiness and self-loathing for having given themselves so easily. For having been used. For not having been truly respected and appreciated. Diana had gotten exactly what she thought she wanted, but she had made one huge mistake: she'd believed that being sexually liberated and owning her sexuality meant having the ability to enjoy casual sex; what she truly wanted was affirmation, acceptance, affection, and the ecstasy of being loved (which is the best ecstasy of all).

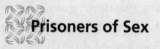 ## Prisoners of Sex

All traditional cultures have been influenced by men because men have traditionally held the positions of authority worldwide. Perhaps because of this fact alone, most organized religions emphasize procreation as the primary reason (and often the only reason) for women to engage in sexual activity. Such edicts are a means of control. Women are seen either as pure or as sluts whose sexual appetite must be suppressed. This confusion between sexuality and morality has done its damage, and it is not surprising that so many women enter adulthood feeling uneasy, embarrassed, uncertain, misinformed, and sinful about sex in general. Many of us were taught that "nice girls" didn't even think about sex before marriage; then, miraculously, sex is supposed to lose all of its nasty connotations and become a joyful experience, as long as it's with your husband.

As children, many of us learned through cultural and religious messages that we shouldn't ask questions about sex or about our private parts. Being female and fearing disapproval, we carefully kept our curiosity a secret. To complicate matters, we learned a false trait of femininity: to depend on others and to seek love from outside. The lesson we learn as girls is that we should learn to adapt and not to make trouble. To be passive is to be loved, even if it means giving up control over our own bodies.

As a reaction to our confusion about our bodies and sexuality, we act out in different ways. Some women, inundated with mixed messages about sexuality, learn to use their bodies and sex as the means to an end. Whether on a subconscious level or not, these women exert power the only way they know how: by aggressively using sex and promises of sex to get what they want. Because they may feel manipulated and powerless by the men in their lives, they make the choice to take advantage of a man's biggest weakness—his desire for sexual pleasure. Other women become totally submissive, virtually ignoring a very important part of what makes a woman who she is: her sexuality. There are varying degrees between these extreme expressions of sexuality and power, which this chapter will help to define. The goal is to help women not only accept themselves but also use their inherent power wisely and compassionately.

The Connection Between Sexuality and Self-Esteem

Owning your sexuality requires sexual self-esteem above anything else. So what is sexual self-esteem? Simply put, sexual self-esteem is a measure of how we feel about our own sexuality; it determines how attractive we feel, how confident we are, how responsive we are sexually, and how free we feel to express our feelings about sex.

Some people (okay, many people) tend not to think of the words "sex" and "self-esteem" as being connected. Nearly everyone engages in sexual activity, and not all of those people (especially women) enjoy a positive self-image. But sexuality and self-esteem are indeed connected, because our sexual experiences are absolutely affected by how high or low our self-esteem is. Nothing is as important to a healthy attitude toward sex as how we feel about ourselves and what we think we deserve. Sexual self-esteem affects perception: how we perceive ourselves and others, how others perceive us, and subsequently, how they treat us.

When we feel good about our sexuality, we are connected to a very powerful part of ourselves. Our sexuality can provide us with a tremendous source of energy and pleasure. Low self-esteem can affect sexuality in a number of ways, though. If you don't feel good about yourself, your sex life may simply be unsatisfying, but it can also be damaging.

Low sexual self-esteem can lead to

- Avoiding sexual relationships because you are afraid of intimacy
- Holding yourself back in sexual relationships because you feel guilty or you don't think you deserve to feel good
- Becoming involved in unhappy or abusive sexual affairs, one after another, because you feel the need to prove your worth (even if only by demonstrating that a man finds you attractive)
- Allowing a man to take advantage of you because you don't believe you deserve to be treated well
- Competing with other women—often friends or relatives—for sexual attention from men
- Judging others through the filter of your own insecurities
- Denying yourself an intimate relationship

Do You Have Low Sexual Self-Esteem?

Ask yourself the following questions:

1. Are you afraid to have sex because you fear your partner will dislike your body?
2. Are you self-conscious about the size of your breasts?

3. Are you worried about stretch marks, scars, or markings that you imagine your sexual partner will be repulsed by?

4. Do you have difficulty reaching orgasm during sex?

5. Do you avoid sex because it reminds you of being sexually abused as a child or raped as an adult?

6. Do you allow your sexual partners to coerce you—even if "only" verbally—into having sex?

7. Do you engage in sexual activities that go against your own morals and cause you shame?

8. Do you have sex with people you do not like or respect?

9. Do you use sex as a way to bolster your ego?

10. Do you have sex even when you don't want to, in order to feel loved?

11. Are you ashamed of your sexual fantasies?

12. Are you insecure about your femininity?

Answering yes to just three of these questions means that you have some work to do before you can enjoy a satisfying and healthy sex life. Sex should be enjoyable, relaxing, loving, comforting, exciting, and self-affirming. Sex can also be something you choose not to engage in for any number of reasons. It is all about getting in touch with what makes you happy, and abstinence is a very valid choice. When a woman doesn't respect herself—when she doesn't love herself enough—she will never enjoy the bliss of being in control of her sexuality, a vital aspect of being a woman. You must love yourself first if you expect to be loved well.

The Truth, the Whole Truth, and Nothing but the Truth!

For women who are struggling with (or simply not thinking about) their own sexuality, there is an obvious place to begin: the truth. Because so many of us are given incorrect and mixed messages about sex, we need to break down the façade and correct erroneous attitudes. Here are some examples of the messages that are still given to some young women. These recurring messages eventually become beliefs and shape our attitudes toward sex in our adult lives. Are any of them familiar?

• Sex is dirty, but not so dirty for men. Sex, in fact, is *good* for the male of our species. Boys are supposed to be sexually curious, and men sexually experienced. Because they are biologically different from women, men have sexual needs that women don't have. It is shameful for a girl to be sexually curious or for a woman to be sexually experienced. In many cultures, girls aren't supposed to want sex or even to have any interest in it until they are married.

• Sex is dirty, and so are the female sexual organs. Male genitalia, by contrast, are magnificent, a source of male pride.

• Sex is dirty, but women can participate in it under two conditions, both within the "sanctity" of matrimony: (1) for the purpose of procreating, (2) to provide pleasure to the husband.

• Sex is dirty, so it's best if women don't enjoy it. But sexual pleasure *is* permissible under certain conditions. A woman can experience sexual pleasure if her husband experiences equal or greater pleasure.

With all of these rules and negative connotations about the female body and female desires, it's no wonder so many women have a hard time connecting with their sexuality. Too often, women are allowed only two options: follow the rules and never truly experience sexual pleasure and freedom, or break the rules and live in shame. Isn't simply living in truth the best option of all? As we know now, when we live in truth, our self-esteem is allowed to blossom, and when we feel good about ourselves, we can fully enjoy being the sexual beings we are, and we can make the wisest decisions for ourselves.

You Don't Have to Be Sexually Active to Be Sexually Aware

Your body and its complexities belong to you and you alone. Choosing to be sexually active is a *choice,* and this decision should never be influenced by outside forces. I learned this important lesson on my own, and it wasn't until I reached the age of thirty that I truly found and understood my own sexuality. That doesn't mean that I remained a virgin until age thirty—I gave birth to my daughter at twenty-eight. But I did not discover or appreciate the fact that I was a "sexual" being until I'd turned thirty. I didn't realize that I was deserving of sexual pleasure, and I didn't learn to love and honor my body and all of its capacities until then. I hadn't yet claimed what was mine.

Throughout my life, I had always felt that "Yasmin" was one entity, and my body was separate from my intellect and emotions. I had always been passionate about life, and I had already made many major discoveries about myself and how I wanted to live. By the time I reached thirty, I did truly own my life, yet I never even thought about owning every part of my body. I never looked at myself in the mirror nude, and thought, You're *fine,* girl! because that would have made me feel dirty and ashamed.

I did not have my first sexual encounter until age nineteen, after being involved with my boyfriend for more than a year. My virginity was sacred to me, and I was not about to give it up easily. Only after an extended period of time, during which he demonstrated that I *was* the queen of his life, and only when I knew that what I felt for him was real love, did I give myself to him sexually. I have no regrets, but I do understand now that I didn't really give myself to him then—or to anyone else—until I was thirty, because I hadn't ever claimed ownership of my body. I didn't *have* myself to give; I just had sex to give. Was my first time fulfilling? Not really—it was more for him than for me. But it was my way of showing him that I loved him. In my twenties, sexual activity with my husband was something I simply did; it wasn't necessarily something that I enjoyed—which had nothing to do with him and everything to do with me. I often thought, Well, either something is wrong with me or this whole sex thing is way overrated. Little did I know that I was wrong on both counts. The real problem was that my beliefs about my body and my sexuality had made me feel that if I loved my body and all the pleasure it could bring me, I would be a tramp.

Through some very intense searching for the truth about what owning my sexuality really meant, I was finally able to break free from the chains of shame. Now when I make a conscious choice to be sexually intimate with a partner, I make it with my mind, heart, body, and soul. I am very discerning about whom I choose as a sexual partner, because I am not only giving my body; I am offering my whole being.

Since my divorce, I have chosen to go through "dry" spells. But just because I am not sexually active for a period of time doesn't mean I've lost ownership of my sexuality. On the contrary, I own my sexuality to the extent that I can share it only with a partner who will honor it the same way I do.

It's very important to recognize, however, that men do not—and will not ever—look at sexuality the same way that women do. For many men, sex is all about physical pleasure; there isn't much that's soulful about it unless they are deeply in love. There are many theories about why that is (which I plan to address in a future book), and circumstances vary, of course, since we are all unique individuals. Certainly, there are women who display a masculine attitude toward sex, but it is a rare woman who can play like the boys and still truly own her sexuality. And who among us wants to, anyway?

Warning

Although I do not address sexual violence in this book, such violence is a scourge that women everywhere, across cultures and social classes, confront every day. There are men who believe that it is their inherent right to have sex with whomever they want, whenever they want—even when a woman chooses to say no. No man—and let me repeat it: no man—has the right to touch you in any way that you do not want him to, even if he's your husband. If you choose at first to have sex with him and then, during sex, change your mind, you have that right. No means no; that's the end of it.

The Attraction-Versus-Affection Dilemma

There isn't a human being on earth who doesn't crave love. It is a basic human need. But we need to be very careful about whom we choose to pursue in that quest for love. We all have our flirtation strategies, and some of our behavior is simply in the genes. Biologically, we are meant to pair up, though some men may stretch the boundaries on how many pairings they can make. If we are confused about what is best for us—because we haven't learned yet how valuable we are—we can make mistakes that are inconvenient at best and destructive at worst. Determining whether you crave attention or real affection will save you a lot of grief.

We all want to feel good about ourselves, and for most women, that includes the desire to look good. Yes, we do it for ourselves, but the real reason we spend so much time and money on our appearance—mostly trying to look sexy—is to appeal to men. So what is it that we really want? Is it the attention we get from being attractive, or is it deeper than that? Among the many women I've met, I've found that many subconsciously attempt to use their sexuality not only to attract men but also to get their affection. The dilemma is that sometimes we are sexy enough to attract a man's *attention,* but then fail to attract his *affection.*

A woman who is sexually attractive will get plenty of male attention, yet few women question whether this is a good thing. Men are attracted in two different ways; I call the first *sexual attraction.* Men are often captured by feminine qualities that promise seduction, pleasure, and bragging rights for the men. And part of this attraction, again, is in the genes; it is a man's biological function to spread his seed. Most men are sexually attracted to the same things we have all been sold on for years: shiny hair, good teeth (believe it or not), full lips, big breasts, and a shapely bottom. It's worth mentioning that the body shapes that men find attractive vary much more widely than we have been led to believe. Although women tend to assume that men prefer thin women, many men say they are most attracted to bigger hips and thighs.

Unfortunately (or maybe it's a blessing in disguise), sexual attraction doesn't produce the results that most of us are looking for, because by itself, it doesn't lead a man to pursue a serious romantic relationship. If the following scenario hasn't happened to you, then it has surely happened to someone you know: A woman relies on her overt sexuality to snare a man, only to find that he uses her once (or maybe on numerous occasions, if she lets him), and then never calls again. He does not consider her a potential life partner. He does not fall in love with her—he just wants to take pleasure in her, and what's more, he'll probably tell all his friends.

Here is a very important truth: sexual attraction causes a man to want to have sex with a particular woman, but that's it. That's all you'll ever realize in a relationship based on sexual attraction alone. You are complicit in your own unhappiness if you rely on the length of your skirt and the color of your lipstick to attract and keep your mate. There is a lack of respect on both sides of the equation. If you play dumb to please a man, or if you give yourself to him sexually in hopes that he'll see what a gem you are, you are making a mistake.

The second type of attraction that a woman might demonstrate is one of *captivation*. When it comes to choosing a partner for the night, a man will choose a sexually attractive woman; if he is looking for a partner for life, he will search for a woman with brains, heart, and humor. She will captivate his mind and his imagination. She will inspire him. All of us, male and female, want to admire and respect our mates; we want to crave time spent with them—in or out of the bedroom. When a woman demonstrates that she can captivate a man, he wants to make her happy, he wants to protect her, and he wants to contribute to her life as a whole. When polled, a group of seven hundred men came up with the following traits when asked to describe what makes a woman "captivating":

- *She is self-confident.* Men like women who like themselves and who are comfortable in their own bodies, whatever their shape or size.
- *She is herself.* Men are sensitive to authenticity. When a woman is perceived to be posing as someone she's not, she is probably dishonest about everything.
- *She has a passion for something.* Whether it's devotion to world peace or to classic films doesn't seem to matter, so long as a woman is passionate about something (not someone) in her life.
- *She is interested in other people.* Men, like women,

prefer to spend time with someone who can listen with as much enthusiasm as she can speak.

- *She needs a man but isn't overly needy.* A woman who can take care of herself but still allows men to contribute to her life is a desirable woman.
- *She likes men.* Each gender has its own traits. A woman should not expect men to be, act, or think just like women. When a woman can appreciate a man's unique qualities, he will appreciate hers.
- *She thinks for herself.* Men don't want a wind-up doll. They want a woman who is confident enough to voice her own opinions without disrespecting someone else's opinions.

In other words, the more you like yourself, the more men will like you. The more you behave authentically, the better chance you'll give men to know you and love you. The more you enjoy your life, the more men will enjoy your company.

What Kind of Woman Are You?

Men respond to women in very powerful and predictable ways, yet femininity is a much more complex issue than most of us realize. Stereotypes abound—the blond bimbo, the dowdy housewife, the shy bookworm, the earth mother—yet all of these concepts are one-dimensional. I'm sure we can all agree that every woman has her own unique and innate feminine qualities. Despite the limitations of stereotypes—and to prove a good point—I have divided the notion of femininity into five stock characters: the Professional, the Little Girl, the Femme Fatale, the Mother, and the Queen. Through these characters, we can more easily recognize our own behavior and its effects on the way people perceive us (and therefore treat us). More important, we'll see that by combining the essence of each character, we can learn what it means to own our sexuality completely.

The Professional

Monica, a twenty-seven-year-old attorney and mother of two, seems by all outward appearances to be a strong, confident, and very intelligent woman. Having broken through most of the negative cultural influences she's grown up with, she appears powerful and in control at work and in her social circle. At home, she is the picture of a loving wife and mother. On the outside, it looks as though Monica has it all.

Monica and I have been friends since childhood. We love each other dearly, but there is one thing we consistently disagree about: our Latino culture's treatment of women. One afternoon, while we were drinking coffee and chatting, Monica said, "Yasmin, I just don't believe in all that oppression stuff. I grew up Latina, and I have lived my life to the fullest. I never internalized any of those submissive messages you talk about. I think that if a woman doesn't like what she learned in the past, then she should just get up and do something about it."

"But most women and girls don't even realize they're being affected by negative cultural stereotypes in the first place," I said.

"How can they not know? That's impossible!" she interrupted.

"Okay, let's put it this way," I began. "As educated, self-aware women, we both recognize the different roles we need to take on at various times. In fact, we usually have the ability to shift into whatever role we need to without even thinking about it. For example, there is Monica the mother, and Monica the attorney. Monica the mommy puts on her mommy hat when she needs to and switches hats when she goes to work."

"I understand—and I agree," she said, smiling.

"Good! Now I'm going to test you." I wanted to demonstrate something I believed Monica had never considered. I stood up and arranged two chairs on different sides of the room. I pointed to the chair on my left and said, "Will Monica the mother please sit here and be Mommy?" She looked at me as if I were crazy, but she played along. She cradled her imaginary babies in her arms, sang a lullaby, and pretended to put them to sleep.

Next, I asked, "Can Monica the lawyer sit in this chair to the right and assume her attorney role?"

She got up, shaking her head at me, and said, "When I argue in court, I always stand. It makes me more powerful." She plucked a notepad from the coffee table and began speaking. Her body language changed. The tone of her voice, even the look in her eye, was very different from Monica the mommy.

Then I asked her, "Can Monica the sexual being please come sit on the sofa?"

Baffled, she stopped in her tracks. She stuttered a little bit, but she couldn't find any words. Then she sat on the couch as if testing its springs. She lay down on her back, and then she sat up again in alarm and cried, "Yasmin, I don't know . . . I don't know who she is. I don't think she even exists!"

I knew not to rush her. Sex is a subject that scares the living daylights out of the strongest of women. I also knew that Monica really believed that she was in touch with herself—that she knew every aspect of her being—yet she had never thought of herself as a sexual entity.

"Of course I have sex with my husband," she said. "But I don't think much about sex at all. I just don't think about . . . pleasure. Sometimes it's okay, and other times I just lie there and wait until he's done. You know, I've never thought of sexuality as an actual part of myself."

Gently, I asked, "So, do you see my point about negative cultural messages and their impact now? You may be the most powerful and self-aware woman I know, yet you're still thinking of your body and its natural needs as secondary. Why do you think that is?"

I'd never seen Monica at a loss for words. It took a moment for her to answer. "Well, now that I think of it, you may be right. I guess I was taught that sex is just something you do with your husband when you get married, and that's that. It's—well, it's an obligation, isn't it? Men need it, and if you don't give it, they'll find it elsewhere. It's part of their nature. And yes, I'm totally in control of my life, but I pretty much ignore those parts between my legs."

I couldn't help bursting out laughing. "Monica, it's called a vagina, and it's every bit as much a part of you as your head! It's your friend, girl."

She turned beet red—something I'd never seen her do before. "It's gonna take me a while, Yasmin. That's all I can say for now."

I knew exactly what to ask her next, because I'd had this discussion with countless women before her: "Tell me the truth. If you were ever to get divorced, do you think your sexuality would cease to exist?"

This time she answered without hesitation. "Yes. I hate to admit that, but I have to be honest with you."

"Would you wish that for your daughter or for your sister—or for me?" I asked.

"No," she said with a hint of a smile. "But no one ever told me anything about my own sexuality. We just didn't discuss that kind of thing!"

"That's my point," I said. "See, even if it's through lying by omission, you, too, have internalized negative messages about your sexuality, and now those messages have become your beliefs. You're missing out!"

"I'll admit it." She laughed, unconvincingly. "I've never, ever thought about it that way." I assured her that most of us don't, because we're never given the chance to explore our opportunities.

There are so many women like Monica out there—women who know how to juggle careers and family with the greatest of ease. She can throw a dinner party together with a day's notice, she can make mincemeat out of her male coworkers, she can attend PTA meetings while conference calling—but she is completely dissociated from her actual physical being. She may hit the gym five times a week, but it's not because she loves her body; it's because she wants to maintain her body so that it can perform.

Monica, who is a perfect example of the Professional, had already broken through many hurdles in her life. She is a fighter who doesn't lack confidence but who lacks self-awareness. She maintains a beautiful body but treats her body as if it were simply something else to take care of, something she would prefer to ignore, even though it makes her what she is: a woman.

The Little Girl

After a seminar I conducted on women and sexuality, I spoke to Lisa, who seemed to be a young woman ready to conquer the twenty-first century by virtue of her go-get-it attitude. She told me a sad and all-too-familiar story, but I was gratified that she was reaching out. Lisa represented what happens when we never allow the little girl inside us to grow up and develop her own feelings about her body and her sexuality. Lisa was still living by unfair and unrealistic standards, passed down through her family and her culture. Luckily, Lisa was self-aware enough to seek help.

"I was taught throughout my childhood that sex is something I should only share with my future husband," she began to tell me. "When I asked my mom about the birds and the bees, she just told me that women who had sexual experiences without being married were sluts." She paused, then continued in a whisper, "I knew something was wrong with that, though, you know? Because my older brother had a string of girlfriends he was obviously having sex with."

"Did you point that out to your mom?" I asked, wondering how comfortable she felt expressing her feelings.

"Well, I tried, but my mom just gave me a look. When I didn't budge, though, she said, 'Men have different needs. That's just the way it is.' So I didn't ask any more questions."

I knew it was important to set Lisa straight, and I

needed a bit more information. She was clearly over the age of twenty, and although I believe a virgin can be every bit as sexually empowered as anyone else, I wanted to make sure the messages she'd received while growing up were not putting her in danger. "Honey, do you mind if I ask if you are sexually active now?"

Her response encompassed the way most women who have taken on the Little Girl persona feel about themselves. "Well, I love my boyfriend a lot. That's not the problem. The thing is . . ." She looked over her shoulder to make sure no one could hear, and continued, "I want to enjoy doing it, I really do, but when we have sex, I get so tense. I feel like my emotions get shut off completely, and I just end up going through the motions to get it over with. When I think about letting myself be free and doing what feels good, I can't help feeling dirty and ashamed. I can't seem to cross the line. In my mind, I know that I am a sexual being and that I have the right to be sexually free, but when the moment comes for me to do it, my body and my emotions are just . . . absent."

I had heard this so many times before—hell, I'd experienced it for myself! "Lisa, I know exactly what you mean," I said.

"You do?" she replied with amazement.

"Of course. The truth is that almost from birth, we have been programmed to believe everything our culture dictates to us about what is proper feminine behavior. When we get older and realize that a lot of those beliefs are wrong, we try to change, but it's so difficult. Shame is really hard to conquer! You can't just will it away, because the seeds were planted a long time ago, and they've taken root deep inside you. Most women don't even realize that they're in a lose-lose situation until they squash those be-liefs and create new ones for themselves. It's not an intellec-tual thing—it goes much deeper than that—and if you continue to deprive yourself of something so important, you're only living half a life." I let that sink in, and then I asked her, "Does your boyfriend treat you the way you want and deserve to be treated?"

She didn't hesitate at all. "Oh, yes. I would never tell him how I really feel about the sex part. It would make him feel bad. He takes wonderful care of me—he's sweet, he buys me gifts all the time, and he says I'm cute and funny. He even says he needs me."

After Lisa and I spoke for a while, I had a lot of hope for her—she was clearly open to self-exploration. She just had to learn some simple truths. First, she had to learn to love her body as much as her man loved it. I was confident that with practice and a patient partner, she would succeed. But she also had to learn that sex cannot be used for any reason other than to simply enjoy the time spent engaging in it. It cannot be used to make a man feel good about him-self or to barter for gifts. It is such an integral part of who you are, you must use it only with great discretion.

Men love the qualities of sweetness and innocence in the Little Girl—it compels them to take care of her. When a woman expresses these characteristics, not only does it make a man feel safe, but it makes him feel masculine. Contrary to popular belief, men need to feel needed, too, and sexually confident women sometimes make men feel threatened and insecure. When the Little Girl comes out, she is both accessible and compliant—she is charming in the truest sense of the word, almost casting a magical spell that makes a man want to please her. Unfortunately, he demonstrates his love in the only way he knows how. He may buy her gifts, he may compliment her, he will protect and defend her, but because she's a Little Girl, he probably won't take her seriously if and when she ever states her demands. Most men will respond to the Little Girl's playful energy with adoration, but unless she can verbalize what she needs, they will remain ignorant as to what brings her real pleasure—on her terms.

As Lisa put on her coat to leave, I added one more thing. "You are obviously an intelligent, beautiful, and caring young woman. I know your boyfriend must appreciate you very much. But it's time for you to see what everyone else sees—a grown woman with needs of her own. Your body and your feelings are complex, and you need to honor that complexity. You're not a little girl any longer, but you don't have to lose her—you just need to help her mature into the passionate, deserving woman you are now."

The Femme Fatale

Think of Jennifer Lopez, and you are thinking of a Femme Fatale—a woman who embodies sensuality and sexuality. In most cases, she relies on her appearance and her confidence to attract men, and she is rarely rejected. This woman's physical energy is not overly aggressive on the outside—it's more like a tickle, an invitation, a warm fire that attracts visitors. She tempts and teases, inviting men to chase her, but she takes the passive role in the pursuit. When a woman expresses this type of feminine energy, men respond; she is almost always described as sexy, regardless of what she is wearing or how she looks. The Femme Fatale seems to effortlessly attract attention, affection, and sexual interest.

All women have the ability to be a Femme Fatale, but it is essential to take this energy on consciously. Women who indiscriminately exude sensuality and sexuality run the risk of being misunderstood as man-eaters. A Femme Fatale who is true to herself will direct her energy in a laserlike fashion at the man of her choice instead of broadcasting it to the world. The truth is, women have the power to use their sexuality to get what they want. This is commonly referred to as the power of seduction. Even young girls learn to use this power—the batting of eyelashes above puppy-dog eyes, sweet baby talk, and lots of "I love you, Daddy" giggles—to manipulate, most often their fathers, even if the goal is a Barbie Dream House or a new dress. As they get older, girls quickly learn that by using their feminine wiles, they can garner attention, favors, and what they mistake for approval from boys. They learn to laugh at the boys' jokes, even those that aren't funny; they engage in physically flirtatious behavior; and much too often, they play dumb in order to play up to the male ego.

It's not as though women plan this behavior; there is no grand scheme we think up when we reach a certain age. Rather, we follow by example. We observe whom we perceive to be the popular girls, and we imitate. The fact is, the power of seduction is as much a part of a woman's natural instinct as it is a man's natural instinct to respond. When a woman recognizes this tool of seduction she owns, she also learns something important: it is a means of power and control. Whereas some women view sex as the most sacred of experiences, others will use their sexuality as a "Scratch my back and I'll scratch yours" barter system.

Not only is this unfair, but it's also unethical. The sexual act is meant to be a moment in time when everything else disappears—it's just you and your partner, enjoying a state of bliss that is unmatched by anything else. When a woman tells a man, "If you buy me that diamond, I'll give you the ride of your life," it cheapens the experience entirely.

There are plenty of women who, perhaps feeling repressed in other areas of their lives, use their sex appeal to make themselves feel powerful. Evidently, these women feel that if they can inspire a man to want to have sex with them, they are in the driver's seat. Make no mistake—the kindest term for this behavior is "manipulation." Rather than building confidence through the development of skills, talents, and smarts, these women derive self-worth from being prized by an external entity. Once a woman uses her looks and her willingness to have sex to control a relationship, once she is "valued" by a man, she feels she can ask for, or even demand, whatever she wants. She may threaten to withhold sex if she feels her desires aren't being sufficiently met. That's when the Femme Fatale persona becomes fatal to a woman's relationship and her self-esteem.

Whether or not we want to accept it, sex is power, and we have an obligation to ourselves to manage that power wisely. Otherwise, we're no better than those who have told us the lies that have influenced us. Your body and your sexuality are a gift to be given and enjoyed—they should never be used as a tool to get what you think you're due.

As women approach their forties, many simply stop expressing any of their positive Femme Fatale qualities. The Femme Fatale is inherently lively, and sometimes we barely have the energy to take care of our daily tasks once we've passed a certain age. As family and career absorb all of our attention, we simply lack the energy needed for the Femme Fatale's fire. In a nutshell, we are just too tired to be sensual or sexual, or even just plain fun. Another reason we don't see many older Femmes Fatales (though there are some very notable exceptions) is that whether or not we become mothers, we begin mothering the men in our lives. We focus more on support than on play and participation, and we lose our zest for fun and adventure, in large part because society makes us feel we are not sexually powerful anymore. While this support is essential to our men, it can make our relationships dull and uninspiring. Also, because acting as the Femme Fatale probably got us into some trouble in our teens and twenties, we may try to suppress her as we mature. We learn our greatest lessons through our mistakes and foibles, though, and the only sensible course is to forgive ourselves and the men involved.

If you have stifled your Femme Fatale and you want to bring her out again, learn to nurture that aspect of yourself. Taking care of your body is an excellent way to begin feeling like a woman at the top of her game again. Work less and sleep more; engage in activities that give you physical pleasure (a massage or bubble bath, for example); practice loving your body, regardless of its shape or size; climb back inside your body instead of dragging it around; express yourself by getting physical (with dancing, yoga, or your favorite sport); and when you have energy, try saving it for play instead of spending it on pleasing others.

By understanding the predictable effects of the Femme Fatale, and by understanding male sexuality, we can "play safe" with this potent feminine energy. Learning to handle your own fire is better than allowing it to be snuffed out.

The Mother

The Mother is the nurturer. Think of . . . your own mother? She embodies patience, faith, belief, caring, healing, serving, comforting, consoling, empathy, and more. The Mother focuses on others' needs, and she always makes the object of her attention feel special. This woman runs a great risk of neglecting herself in favor of just about anyone else.

Men are often accused of looking for a mother. My answer: Wouldn't you? I haven't outgrown my own need for nurturing, and I don't believe I ever will. We women are usually fortunate enough to have friends and family with motherly qualities, and we often take them for granted. What we don't fully appreciate is that nurturing is a distinctly feminine trait—few men can count on such support from their male friends and family.

As is the case with the Femme Fatale and the Little Girl, men respond to the Mother in predictable ways. The Mother makes a man feel cared for. She provides a safe haven from the hardships of life, and she helps boost her man for the next adventure or battle. The woman with motherly qualities strengthens a man's spirit, her attention and ministrations renew him, the food she prepares warms his belly, and her encouragement warms his soul.

It's very important to distinguish between the wonderful feminine qualities I refer to as belonging to the Mother and mothering itself. In too many instances, mothering is really just a sneaky way to force advice, food, and opinions on our men, making them feel like children. Men find this behavior emasculating and (surprise!) a huge turnoff. The major difference between mothering and assuming the

Mother character is control. The Mother offers her qualities as gifts, allowing the receiver to remain in control. The woman who uses mothering as a means of control dominates thoughts and actions, which isn't fair to anyone.

Most men consider the nurturing qualities of the Mother a requirement in a wife, and when they begin searching in earnest for a life partner, they naturally start looking for women who display such traits, as opposed to the days when they simply craved sex and excitement (the Femme Fatale). Men know that the better they are cared for, the more successful they will be. The cliché that behind every successful man is a supportive woman is usually true. The adoration the Femme Fatale inspires is no substitute for the long-term care and comfort that the Mother provides.

Beware: one of the Mother's qualities is self-sacrifice, which in many ways is a blessing, or none of us would have survived infancy! But without boundaries, the Mother will sacrifice anything for anyone, even if it's not in her best interests. Without self-esteem and self-respect, the Mother will always put other people's needs first. What's more, she will feel the obligation to nurture anyone who crosses her path, which is not only inappropriate but also exhausting!

The Queen

The Queen is rare. Think Oprah. She has vision and purpose; she is generous and serene. She is concerned with empowerment—specifically, the ability to give power without losing it. She has a unique ability to understand other people, and perhaps most important, she has an enormous capacity to receive. She is influential and powerful in a uniquely feminine way.

While the Mother focuses on serving individuals, the Queen focuses on a group I call her realm. It is a realm she defines for herself because her boundaries and her self-esteem are so strong. She does not give away her greatness; rather, she shares it in hopes that those around her will realize their own greatness. In contrast to the Mother, who focuses on what people need, the Queen pays attention to the quality and future of life within her realm. The Queen's noble purpose is her vision and may include hopes for freedom, self-expression, vitality, and integrity. It is what she has in her own life, and it is what she passionately wants people to have in their lives, too. The Queen's existence serves a loftier purpose, which is why others serve her. Both genders naturally find themselves attracted to a woman with queenly qualities because she inspires respect and admiration. Hers are the feminine qualities that make a man strive to be the best man he can be—her recognition empowers him, giving him the energy and daring to attempt ever larger feats.

The best term to describe the way men respond to the Queen is that they become her "provider," and because men are natural providers, most of them are looking for someone who is worthy and able to receive their gifts. There are many things men seek to provide for their Queen, and those things certainly aren't limited to material goods. They will try to provide her with whatever they perceive she needs, they will do what they think will make her happy, they will support her purpose, and if an opportunity arises, they will help her to realize her vision.

Because the Queen inspires men to provide, most women would strive to be like her all of the time. But it's wise to pursue a much more balanced approach to femininity. If you can identify with and embrace all five of the feminine characters and make room for each of them in your life and relationships, you will be more satisfied, more independent, and more cherished and respected. Men provide for the Queen, but they participate with the Femme Fatale; they get the nurturing they need from the Mother, but they prove their masculinity with the Little Girl.

The Professional is unique in this group: in many ways, she embodies all of the qualities that make a woman great. She is powerful and in control, she is successful and confident, she always gets the job done and commands admiration, she has the respect of everyone around her. But she's missing one element that is crucial to her happiness— her sexuality. In some of the same ways as the Mother, she is so busy running her world that she has lost the ability to listen to her own body. The Professional would do well to discover the Femme Fatale within her.

I would never suggest that a woman change her personality unnaturally, especially to please a man. We are all born to be our own, unique selves. But we can learn from these female archetypes by analyzing their strengths and weaknesses and incorporating the best of their characteristics. We can combine aspects of each of these women in order to strengthen our resolve to seek what we want and what we need. Remember, you are in control; the way you are treated is a direct result of how you are perceived.

Creating a New Belief System About Your Sexuality

For many women, sexuality constitutes the last frontier of self-acceptance and self-love. Women describe themselves as loving mothers and wives and even competent professionals, yet when asked about their sexuality, many of them express self-doubt and shame. The mere mention of sex is taboo in most traditional households; the topic is simply not discussed. Girls learn early on that sex, for them at least, is something to be hidden, something to be frightened of, but something they are duty-bound to perform when they marry. The sexual messages that are conveyed in these households revolve around fear, control, self-loathing, and shame; they very rarely encourage women to experience pleasure or gratification with a man, let alone by themselves. No one is born thinking sex is bad or good; rather, the environment we grow up in defines how our sexuality will manifest itself. Even apparently self-assured women often deny themselves a fulfillment that everyone deserves. We were all given bodies capable of experiencing pleasure. Why should half of us feel ashamed to enjoy it, or even to think about it?

I'd like to offer you an alternative to the belief system you may have been influenced by—one I've incorporated myself. You, too, can learn to overcome all of the damaging messages that have muzzled you, and you can enjoy everything about your own sexuality and what makes you happy. Once you are able to recognize that you are the master of your own feelings and that sex is a gift to be enjoyed, you can discover what it feels like to be free.

How do we change imposed beliefs that we know are not good for us? By acknowledging those beliefs and understanding where they came from, how they were developed, and how they have affected our self-esteem, as we have explored in this chapter. We also need to understand that our feelings about our bodies and our sexuality are not entirely accessible by intellect. In fact, many of us store our feelings in our bodies and our subconscious minds, making it difficult to reach and eliminate them.

To borrow from the philosophy of Alcoholics Anonymous, it's most important to admit that you are powerless to change your beliefs about sexuality through intellect alone. You must recognize the damage already done, if that's the case, and admit that you are not living the sexually healthy life that you deserve. Next you must learn to channel your own instincts, your higher power, and your knowledge of your own body. Acknowledging that your higher power always wants what is best for you is a very positive step toward getting in touch with your sexuality.

Finally, you must make a conscious decision to turn to your own divine wisdom for guidance. This step bypasses the intellect entirely—it is a leap of faith and an acknowledgment that you know what is best for yourself under any circumstances. By relying on your inner wisdom, you can remove harmful beliefs and replace them with healthy ones, because they come *from* you, *for* you.

Ultimately, you must feel that you deserve more. If you perceive pleasure as something dirty, nothing will change. It's also imperative that you get in touch with your own body, both figuratively and literally (the exercises in Chapter Eight will help you). Understanding and accepting the way you are now—that is, how your mind has been influenced through upbringing and experience, and how your body looks and feels—is a very important step toward understanding and accepting your own unique, worthy sexual nature.

The much desired female body is, and always has been, considered a great prize. Men instinctively seek out a mate by whatever means of evaluation they've been brought up to follow. It is up to us as women to choose who will get this prize. In the end, we really are the power wielders when it comes to sex, and that's why it is so important not to use that power to manipulate. The wisest women will hold out until a man proves he is worthy; if we are foolish enough to be easily impressed by false attraction, we will never give ourselves the opportunity to experience true affection—and the results can be disastrous.

Many of us were brought up to believe that an experienced woman who knows a lot about sex is a slut. Nothing could be further from the truth. Knowledge is power, and one of the greatest gifts you can give yourself is the confidence that comes from owning your sexuality and making choices that are right for you.

6
WHO CAN STOP
YOU NOW?

> You can learn new things at any time in your life if you're willing
> to be a beginner. If you actually learn to like being a beginner,
> the whole world opens up to you.
>
> **—Barbara Sher, author of *It's Only Too Late If You Don't Start Now:***
> ***How to Create Your Second Life at Any Age***

Self-respect lays the groundwork for true success because without it, your success will never be real. Success will be externalized, centered on outside sources, instead of on your internal integrity. True success is a feeling that cannot be taken or given by the outside world. It is not defined by the car you drive or the house you live in or how much money you make. True success is the ability to live a fulfilling life as defined by you. It is knowing yourself well enough to realize that no matter what blow life may strike you with, your character will remain constant.

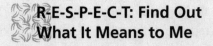R-E-S-P-E-C-T: Find Out What It Means to Me

We develop our first concepts of respect in our early home environment, and we carry those impressions with us for the rest of our lives. When I was growing up, my girl-friends and I were taught by our parents to be *mujercitas educadas,* educated young women. This had nothing to do with schooling but referred to character and acceptable be-havior—being respectful, polite, and obedient and display-ing good manners. There were many unwritten rules about what an "educated" girl was supposed to do. Aside from the common characteristics of being *educada,* such as say-ing "please" and "thank you," the most important virtue was showing respect—respect for your elders, above all. An unfortunate notion in many cultures is that regardless of whether a woman is twelve, twenty-two, or forty-two, she is expected to respect anyone born before her, simply be-cause they have lived longer and supposedly know better. She is also expected to listen to and abide by her elders' opinions about how she should act, what she should say, and whom she should associate with—in essence, *who she should be.*

So what do we do when we hear an elder or a supe-rior make a comment about us that we don't agree with? Shouldn't we enjoy the freedom to be honest and say that although we respect this person, we don't believe that what he or she is saying is accurate? Aren't we worthy enough to have and voice our *own* opinions respectfully? And if the answer to these questions is yes, why are so many women constantly being criticized about how they behave when they disagree? Too many of us have been led to believe that we're being disrespectful if we say how we really feel. Ex-pressing yourself, whether to an elder, a supervisor, or a spouse, is not disrespectful. It's when we don't speak up that we are showing disrespect—for ourselves.

During one of my seminars, I asked a group of Latina

women and girls whether they had been taught the supposed virtue of showing respect at home. Without hesitation, they shouted in unison, "Yes!"

Sabrina said, "I was taught never to say anything back to my elders, that it is very disrespectful."

Ana, her sixteen-year-old daughter, agreed: "I have to respect all of my older relatives, even if they don't respect me. My father told me that maybe someday they'll pay me the same respect, but for now I have to do the right thing and show deference, no matter what. Talking back is a really serious offense in my house, even when I'm trying to be polite." Her mother simply nodded in agreement, as if it were absolutely normal.

I asked the group what they thought about this dilemma. A woman in her mid-twenties replied, "I don't even think about it; that's just the way it is."

Another teenager added, "It's a family thing. All the relatives help one another take care of the kids; therefore the kids have to respect everyone as if they were our parents."

She'd made a very important point. In Latino culture, and in most traditional societies, it is customary for the extended family to assist in raising, educating, and disciplining one another's children. An aunt, uncle, or even a cousin may have a say in a child's upbringing. Unfortunately, extended-family discipline is often taken too far. Because women are taught to respect their elders no matter what, they are subjected to insults from any number of adults and extended-family members, with no recourse. This violates a young woman's self-respect and whittles away at her self-confidence. Ultimately, someone with low self-esteem starts believing that it is appropriate and natural to be mistreated.

Too often, the way our elders treat us encourages our own negative self-image, and diminishes our own ability to love ourselves. How can girls grow into self-respecting women when they are treated with contempt from such a young age?

As women, we must recognize that this cultural definition of respect is false and that true respect is a two-way street. It breaks my heart when I see women in their thirties and forties still allowing themselves to be diminished by their families. These women continue to struggle to stand up for themselves when dealing with people outside the home, too, including friends, boyfriends, coworkers, and bosses. Because they have been conditioned so well, some women never learn the skill of simply asking for what they need and want, nor do they learn to simply say no. If we want to be taken seriously, we need to demonstrate strength and conviction, and we can best achieve that by drawing lines in the sand.

Boundaries Demand Respect

Healthy relationships are all about boundaries and are nourishing and functional. Our relationships are particularly likely to be unhealthy and dysfunctional if they are too close or too distant, too rigid or too loose. Because men establish boundaries in most cultures, women never have an opportunity to create their own, and women with no boundaries allow people to infiltrate their lives inappropriately. These women have difficulty determining when a matter is none of someone else's business. As a result, they lack privacy in thought, emotions, and physical space.

When our boundaries are well defined, we are healthier as individuals and as partners in any type of relationship. Boundaries set limits on what is safe and appropriate for us to feel; they restrict what we allow to "get" to us; and they remind us of what we can rise above. Boundaries determine how we let people treat us, and it is critical that we establish these limits in all areas of our lives. Family boundaries help us recognize where the family ends and where we as individuals begin, and we cannot hope to realize our full potential if we don't embrace our own identities. When we make the decision to make and play by our own rules, attitudes change—you'll see. When we learn to ignore gratuitous criticism from our families, to tune out the comments we know don't apply to us, family members will begin to treat us differently, more respectfully. When we demonstrate strength instead of acquiescence in a courteous but righteous manner, we'll find that we really can control how we are treated, not just by our families but by the world.

Most women really do want to put an end to the disrespect that's heaped upon them; they just don't know how. Although intellectually we may believe that it's correct to stand up for ourselves, no one ever told us that we had the right to act on this idea. We've only been told what we *can't* do, with no explanation. As a result, we're left knowing that disrespect is wrong, but we don't know why. One way women try to hide their shame in allowing this disrespect in their lives is by minimizing it, and therefore allowing it to continue. The reality is that, as much as we try to minimize disrespect, it will *always* affect us subconsciously, causing us to doubt ourselves. We must value ourselves enough to believe that we are worth standing up for.

Simply stated, it is crucial for you to claim your self-respect and to acknowledge the consequences if you can't or won't. Once you can create your own boundaries, you will be better equipped to define what is and what is not acceptable in your life. We deserve to be treated with respect by all of the people in our lives—including our parents and other family members—regardless of their age. We must demonstrate through our actions that there are certain lines that we will not tolerate being crossed. Remember: you always have the right to say, "Please don't speak to me that way." Most women have a hard time with that concept. Why? Because we feel we're unworthy of better treatment; we actually feel that we don't have the right to ask for respect. Even if a relative tells us that we are misguided or stupid or weak, why can't we look that person in the eye and, with a sense of calm inner power and assurance, say, "Actually, I'm not. If you think so, that's your opinion. Please don't disrespect me again by speaking that way to me." The trouble deepens when we become so accustomed to allowing family members to speak to us in a negative manner that this tolerance carries over into other areas of our lives. That's when our boundaries will save us or sink us, repress us or make us irrepressible.

Setting boundaries for yourself means taking responsibility, being an adult, and demanding equality and respect. It means drawing a line on the sand and saying, "You can't put a toenail past this"—saying *no* to things that are wrong for you, no matter what happens, where you are, or whom you're with. The need for boundaries emerges from a deep sense of our own personal rights, especially the right to be who we are. As we learn to value, trust, and listen to ourselves, and when we take risks and make important decisions, our boundaries become sharper and stronger over time.

Respect: it's your birthright, you deserve it, and you must claim it, beginning at home and extending to all aspects of your life.

Claiming Respect in the Business World

"Respect is not given; it is earned." Sounds good, right? In fact, it is just an excuse that people use to justify treating others with disrespect. Respect is your birthright; you may claim it from anyone at any time. Everyone deserves a certain level of respect simply for being human. There is never an excuse for someone to disrespect you, nor is there ever an excuse for you to disrespect anyone.

People in a professional setting will often try to rationalize their disrespect. After graduating from college, I went to work for a consulting firm. Before my first session with the managers and several corporate vice presidents of a well-known shipping company, I was sitting with the president of my firm and our guests. At one point, one of our clients said, "I don't understand what the big deal is about calling people Hispanic or Latino. I'm afraid to call them either because they might get offended."

"I understand," I told him gently before describing the nuances of the various Hispanic communities.

In the middle of my explanation, my boss nudged me and said out loud, "No, Yasmin." I looked at her with confusion and continued to speak. Once again, she rudely interrupted me and said, "Why don't we just discuss the goals we have for today's class?"

I was furious—she had blatantly disrespected me. Regardless of whom she'd disrespected me in front of, she had no right to speak to me that way. "Dr. Johnson," I said quietly, "can I speak to you for a moment in private?"

"Your class is about to start. Can't it wait until the end of your session?" she asked.

"No, it can't," I responded. I took Dr. Johnson into the hallway and said, "I must tell you, I don't appreciate the way you just disrespected me."

"What are you talking about?" she demanded.

"The way you rudely shut me up out there is unacceptable to me. I definitely don't deserve to be treated that way."

"Yasmin, you have not earned your place yet. You can't just give your opinion as you wish. This client doesn't know you, and you have to earn their respect first."

"I understand that. But I still believe the way you handled the situation was wrong. If you had a problem with what I said, you could have asked to speak to me outside the room."

"But this is a big client!" Dr. Johnson said, trying to defend herself for being disrespectful.

"That may be, and as the president of this company, you have a responsibility to keep this client, but not at the expense of disrespecting me," I explained.

"I'm sorry, Yasmin," she said, surprisingly embarrassed. "You're right. I should have handled the situation differently. Now, can we get back to class? These corporate managers are waiting for you."

I went on to teach a successful seminar, but it was the

last class I taught for Dr. Johnson. Shortly thereafter, I turned in my resignation. Although she apologized for her behavior, my boss was known for treating employees with disrespect. If I'd stayed at the firm, it would simply have been a matter of time before she disrespected me again, and I knew, even then, that if I allowed others to mistreat me in any way, I was giving myself a subconscious message of unworthiness. I knew, even then, that respect is a two-way street, and if the people I worked with didn't want to play by rules I considered fair and reasonable, then I would remove myself from their game.

The Empowered Woman

What are the secrets of women who are at the top of their game and who feel no shame in claiming their position?

These women know that guilt is a game they can choose not to play; they have an intimate knowledge and a love of themselves; they assert their will in creating their own lives, on their terms; and they know that self-respect equals power. What do you call these everyday heroes of their own lives, who are truly living life as they choose? I call them irrepressible spirits. A woman who is in control of her life has certain characteristics and strategies that allow her to excel at whatever she does:

- She does not compromise her self-respect.
- She is not held back by past hurts, mistakes, or shame.

- She uses fear as fuel to propel herself into greatness.
- She fully expresses both her power and her vulnerability.
- She knows how to live, love, work, and play with all her heart.
- She has developed tools to cover any situation with any person.
- She has the courage to uncover her full potential.
- She has created an original plan to achieve all of her goals.

Irrepressible women break through barriers and knock down walls. When they want something badly enough, there is nothing in the world they won't do—so long as it is not illegal, cruel, or hurtful—to get it. These women overcome fear, doubt, and often great adversity to achieve what the rest of the world may see as an impossible goal. Where some of us see only our limitations, these women move forward with courage, exploring new worlds, achieving great dreams, and ignoring warnings that "it" can't, or shouldn't, be done. No obstacle is too great for a woman with an irrepressible spirit.

Developing into a powerful woman is a process. Before we can achieve, we must believe that we deserve to achieve. Sometimes that is very difficult, because we've been brought up with mixed—and often incorrect—messages about our place in life. If we are not treated with respect as girls, we have to work hard to replace our own negative beliefs about ourselves with positive ones. To be repressed is to be stifled and smothered; to be irrepressible, you must love yourself enough to allow the real you to blossom, even if you have critics.

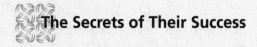

The Secrets of Their Success

An article in the *Harvard Business Review* claimed that in the 1970s, women succeeded the only way they could: by imitating the qualities and characteristics associated with their male colleagues. Today, though, many women are discovering that while it's helpful to learn the games their mothers never taught them, they don't have to follow conventional wisdom about the way people in power positions should act, think, or lead. Instead, more and more women are doing what comes naturally: trusting themselves to create their own paths by developing their own rules of the game. The women whose quotes below identify ten vital "secrets" represent every walk of life, but they have all respected themselves and their own unique attributes. If you can incorporate these lessons into your life, you, too, can become an irrepressible spirit.

Secret #1

Successful women don't play it safe—especially when they see a risky choice as their only choice.
—Barbara Olson, the U.S. assistant attorney who died aboard the plane that crashed into the Pentagon on September 11, 2001

Taking risks is so difficult because there are never any guarantees. Fear of the unknown can hold back even the most courageous among us, but because risk is integral to success, taking informed and calculated chances is absolutely necessary. Consider the following tips:

- Don't focus on the negative. Instead, consider all of the possible benefits. You'll never reach the top of the mountain if you're always looking down.

- Weigh the pros and cons. It doesn't make sense to risk a lot for what may be a small potential gain. Ask yourself, Exactly what am I likely to win by taking this risk? What are the realistic chances of success? What could I win or lose, either by going ahead or by standing still?

- Welcome fear, but never allow it to immobilize you. Use your gut feelings to increase your awareness, regardless of the situation. Fear should act as a helpful warning, but not as a barrier to moving forward.

- Get all the facts, and make sure your facts are accurate. The more you know about a situation, the better you can evaluate the risk involved.

- Examine the worst-case scenario. Many times, you'll find that it's not nearly as bad as you'd first imagined.

Secret #2

Play like a man until you can change the rules.
—Gail Evans, CNN executive vice president and bestselling author

In her book *Play Like a Man, Win Like a Woman,* Gail Evans shares advice on how to compete in a male-dominated society and come out on top. Evans began working for CNN when it was founded in 1980, at a time when female broadcast journalists were synonymous with beautiful TV anchorwomen. By 1996 she was executive vice president for the pioneering cable news channel, because she knew how to play like a man until she could mold her own version of the corporate world.

Whatever arena you choose to get into, you need to understand the existing playing field, even if you eventually choose to make up your own game. Evans recounts the story of Red Cross president Bernadette Healy. Healy, a cardiologist, paid her dues and rose through the ranks of the National Institutes of Health (NIH), achieving the position of president in 1991. Just two weeks later, she officially announced the creation of a Women's Health Initiative. Up until then, NIH research had been focused on men and their diseases. Grant funds were used to test drugs and other treatments primarily on male subjects. Remarkably enough, even a study on estrogen and heart attacks was conducted only with men! It's little surprise that very few women sat on the review panels that approved these studies. Healy's Women's Health Initiative eventually produced a radical shift in the way research was funded. It took a tremendous effort to change anything within the academic and research bureaucracies, but Healy succeeded in creating her own agenda.

Evans and Healy demonstrate a truth that many professional women will eventually have to acknowledge: we still live in a male-dominated society, and in order to succeed, we need to manipulate the system from the inside. It's okay to play by men's rules and win. What's even better is when you can decide the rules yourself.

Secret #3

Sometimes it's not enough to simply knock on doors. You've gotta knock them down!
—**Marion Luna Brem, author of *Women Make the Best Salesmen* and *The 7 Greatest Truths About Successful Women***

When she was a thirty-year-old mother of two, Marion Luna Brem was given some of the most devastating news any person can hear: she had cancer, with a life expectancy of two to five years. Brem had no job and no health insurance, and her most pressing concern was how to pay the next month's rent. She describes this period of her life as "the definition of a living nightmare." She had no choice but to fight, however, if only for her children. First she had to find work to pay for treatment. "You've always been good with people. Why don't you try sales?" her best friend suggested. Little did Brem know that she would end up running her own successful business empire.

After sixteen fruitless interviews, she landed a job selling cars. Twelve weeks into the job, she was named salesperson of the month, and by the end of her first year, a plaque was mounted on the office wall proclaiming Brem salesperson of the year. Four and a half years after selling her first car, and with her cancer in remission, she bought her own dealership. In the next decade, doors of opportunity flung wide open as she embraced her irrepressible drive and expanded her franchise. What makes this self-made woman such a powerhouse?

- Persistence
- Resilience

Persistence and resilience are two of the most important elements of success. Persistence will keep you moving forward, and resilience will help you bounce back when things don't go as planned. None of us control where we come from, nor can we allow ourselves to remain stagnant if we have dysfunction in our lives. What we *can* do is begin moving past what stands in our way. When we truly know how much potential we have, we embrace the idea of taking chances because we know that with each attempt, we are one step closer to unlocking the doors to success.

Persistence means not taking no for an answer; it means challenging norms and other people's opinions and having complete faith in yourself to decide the course of your life. Without persistence, Brem's life would have taken a far different turn. Her message is: you must believe in yourself enough to fight for what you need.

Some people believe resiliency is something you are either born with or not. I disagree. I believe, as does Brem, that your capacity for resilience is not genetically fixed, nor are there any limits to how resilient you can become. Increasing resilience is all about changing the way you think about adversity. Research has shown that resilience is key to success and happiness in all areas of life because it demonstrates the degree of control that one has over one's life. You can teach yourself to be resilient with the help of the exercises in Chapter Eight. Once you allow yourself to be strong—to be a thriving survivor rather than a victim—you can profoundly change the way you handle setbacks and approach obstacles. Resilience transforms hardship into challenge, failure into success, and helplessness into power. As Brem says it herself, "Courage is not a gift; it is a decision."

Secret #4

A person who has a strong enough "why" can bear almost any "how."

—Yrma Rico, author, founder of Entravision

Purpose is the fuel that ignites irrepressible spirits. When difficult situations come our way, women using their power of purpose can propel themselves past almost any obstacle. Women with purpose don't allow anyone or anything to stop them from achieving their goals.

The path Rico is describing is the W.I.T. Road: doing "whatever it takes." Following that road enables us to turn problems into opportunities. It helps us to understand that it's not what actually happens to us that matters; it's what we do with what we are given that determines our quality of life. While many of us create "blame lists" to assuage our frustration, deep down we know that we, and we alone, are responsible for our circumstances. It is up to us to take control of the quality of our lives, and to do so, we must find our purpose. Once found, this purpose ignites passion, which is powerful energy indeed. When you are passionate about what you do, it's not the destination that matters so much as the journey. Without passion and purpose, it's nearly impossible to sustain the high level of energy and interest that you need in order to do "whatever it takes." The choice is yours: you can choose to live your life to the fullest, getting in touch with your purpose and pursuing activities that ignite your passion, or you can choose to live a mediocre life as an observer rather than a participant. We are all capable of achieving greatness, but only after we recognize the greatness in ourselves.

Secret #5

Mistakes are part of the dues one pays for a full life.
—Sophia Loren, actress

Irrepressible women do not see mistakes as failures. Instead, they see mistakes as opportunities to learn and develop new skills and life strategies. Failure implies waste, as if nothing has been gained, yet it is through failure that people gain the most knowledge about themselves, about others, and about life. Mistakes are inevitable, but turning would-be failures into learning experiences is essential to success of any kind. I firmly believe that the more mistakes you make, the greater depth of knowledge you gain. Irrepressible women understand that each mistake brings them one step closer to achieving their dreams. They do not wallow in self-pity or frustration, because those feelings gain these women nothing. They make amends or solve problems, analyze the situation thoroughly, and move on with a stronger mind, heart, and soul. We cannot learn to get up and run until we've experienced the frustration of falling down—sometimes over and over again. Understanding that frustration only makes us stronger. The only time a mistake is a true failure is when it deters us from our goals and breaks our spirits.

Secret #6

Believe in yourself, and there will come a day when others will have no choice but to believe with you.
—Iyanla Vanzant, author and self-help specialist

"I love myself so much," Iyanla Vanzant said at one of her packed seminars. "I love myself because I know God made me in the perfect image of himself. I'm the one that drives myself crazy sometimes trying to be all-perfect. You see, the difference between all of you out there and me," she continued, "is that I know I'm crazy, and I accept and believe in my crazy self. All of you out there keep trying to be perfect and do not realize that it is your imperfections that make you so perfect. So stop trying to convince others that you are great and learn to truly believe that you are great!"

You cannot ask others to believe in you if you don't believe in yourself. We all know that's true in theory, but we forget to apply it to our daily lives. Too often we wait for cues from others before we realize the value of who we are. The problem is that we cannot wait around for others to see the true glory in us before we recognize it ourselves. We have a responsibility to ourselves, and that is to believe in ourselves first. Along with the exercises found in Chapter Eight, consider the following:

- You need to believe that what you think, feel, and desire is as important as what others think, feel, and desire. Say without apology: "I want, I prefer, I choose, I desire, I [fill in the blank]." Then stick by it!
- Take personal responsibility for your own life. You must learn to be comfortable with your own power, never apologetic, never halfhearted, and never engaged in blame.
- Be the most authentic "you" you can be. People respect and admire individuals who live in truth and are honest about themselves. That means loving and admiring yourself with all of your imperfections.

Secret #7

The willingness to accept responsibility for one's own life is the source from which self-respect springs.
—Oprah Winfrey

We live in a blaming society. We cope with unpleasant situations and feelings by faulting everyone—from our parents to the government to the tooth fairy. Irrepressible women refuse to buy into the mentality that says "I could succeed if it weren't for _____."

Empowered women realize that when you place the responsibility for your failures on someone else or another outside force, you are preventing yourself from succeeding. You are literally giving away your power by demonstrating that someone has more control over your life than you do. Irrepressible women don't buy into this victim mentality. You must understand that there are certain things in life you can't control, such as nature, the past, and other people. There are also things you absolutely can control, such as your thoughts, your actions, and your opinion of yourself. Taking responsibility for your life is the most empowering thing you can do—and here are three steps you can begin practicing right now that will help you on your way:

- Make a detailed analysis of the values and opinions offered by others, and then mold those views to fit your own vision of what you want.
- Make yourself the cause and effect. Don't demand that someone else "do something" while you wait around and suffer.
- Realize that independence and personal responsibility are the main ingredients of personal power.

Secret #8

Do not follow where the path may lead. Go instead where there is no path and leave a trail.

—Selena, the late celebrated singer-songwriter

In life, Selena was the queen of Tejano music. In death, the twenty-three-year-old singer became a legend. Although she didn't speak much Spanish as a child, she spoke enough to become the biggest star of the Tejano genre, crossing the divide between traditional Mexican songs and the nearly impenetrable realm of American pop. By her late teens, Selena was a household name in Mexico and much of the rest of Latin America; by the time of her tragic death, she was on the verge of an unprecedented position on the U.S. music charts. She stole the hearts of Mexican Americans by giving them a face and a voice they could be proud of.

So how was this young woman able to create such a legacy in such a short time? Because she was different. Selena forged an entirely new path. If you can already see your path laid out in front of you, one thing is clear: it is not your path. Every woman is a unique and powerful individual with the ability to either follow in the footsteps of others or create the path that is best suited for her. Your own path is created during moments of action, not by following what came before you. Yes, that's a scary thought! But because we all have our own strengths and gifts, it only makes sense that we should chart our own course. We are made to share our special talents—whatever they may be— with the world. To discover your path by listening to your heart is to live with purpose.

Secret #9

The truth will set you free, but first it will piss you off.
—Gloria Steinem, political and social activist

The truth can irritate, frustrate, and anger you because facing the truth seems much more difficult than living a lie. Sooner or later, though, the truth is inescapable, and that's a blessing in disguise. Telling the truth to yourself and to others is infinitely liberating. Once you acknowledge the truth—particularly about something that bothers you—you can finally begin to do something about it. As they say in AA, once you admit that you are powerless over an addiction, you can begin to treat it. Denying a problem only makes it worse. There is great meaning in the saying "You are only as sick as your secrets."

Living in truth means seeing things for what they really are. It means rejecting denial. Many times, as wives, friends, or mothers, we tend to idealize our own lives, making them into what we think others want to see. Living in denial sets us up to be victims of our own creation. Sometimes we don't understand why things happen to us or why certain situations end up the way they do. If we can identify the root of any given problem, we can ascertain whether its foundation has been built on truth or falsehoods.

Although it sounds contradictory, we always know, even if only at a subconscious level, when we are living in denial. It's just that we usually ignore the truth because we are somehow invested in maintaining the lies we have built our world around.

- Living in truth is not the same as always telling the truth—it goes much deeper.
- Living in truth means never lying to yourself.
- Living in truth means becoming aware of when you lie, why you lie, and whom you lie to, and correcting that behavior.
- The decision to begin the process of living in truth is itself a decision of will.

Secret #10

I've been popular and unpopular, successful and unsuccessful, loved and loathed, and I know how meaningless it all is. Therefore, I feel free to take whatever risks I want.
—Madonna, performer and entrepreneur

Whether you love or loathe her, there's no denying that Madonna lives life as she chooses, and she is wildly successful. That's because she realizes that no matter what she does or doesn't do, there will always be critics. What this irrepressible woman has learned very well is that each of us has our own model of our own world. No one model is right or wrong; they are all just different. When we learn to accept that our own model of the world might not be someone else's, our burden is lightened. Our expectations are our own, and we have no one to please but ourselves. We may even develop compassion for those critics!

We expend too much energy trying to change people into what we believe is right for them. We waste so much time and emotion judging others that we forget how precious our differences are. When you can break away from the pressure of feeling judged yourself, you achieve real freedom. When you no longer rely on the praise of others for your self-worth, you gain the ability to go out on a limb.

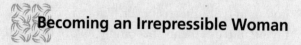 **Becoming an Irrepressible Woman**

Trusting that you'll be able to deal with the outcome of any uncertain situation is the foundation for overcoming fear.

Everything else is built on top of it, so your base had better be sturdy. If you do not have faith in the process of facing the unknown with peace of mind, you will give up every time something goes wrong. When we live with the worry of uncertainty, we waste time and energy desperately searching for answers. I know—I've been there and done that, too. What we must understand is that the answers we seek can usually be found inside ourselves—there's no reason to seek them elsewhere. When you're standing up to uncertainty, you need to trust yourself—your instinct, your guts, your higher power, your experiences, your beliefs, and your smarts.

Life is all about the journey, not the destination. Your experiences today will help you make decisions about your tomorrow. The beauty of uncertainty is that once you can outwit it by providing your own answers, you'll no longer see the unknown as scary; it will become a challenge you relish. When you trust yourself enough to create your own answers, you end up creating your own world, the way you want it. This freedom allows you to blossom, whether you are opening your own business, moving out of your father's home, or accepting a position in the highest echelons of power. We either take control of our lives or let life take control of us.

As you have seen throughout the pages of this book, you are not alone. Many women have gone through tragedies and setbacks and overcome them. You, too, can become an irrepressible woman with an unstoppable spirit if you remember:

- Always claim your self-respect.
- Don't be afraid to take risks.

- Persevere and be resilient.
- Learn the rules, and then make them your own.
- Embrace the unknown and accept it as a challenge.
- Turn your mistakes into learning experiences.
- Silence the critics, especially if you are your own worst critic.
- Find your purpose and dedicate yourself to it with passion.
- Commit yourself to doing whatever it takes.
- Love and believe in yourself, imperfections and all.

The most important piece of advice I can offer you is to proactively and confidently search for answers within yourself when you are faced with decisions. Because each person is unique, what works for me may not work for you. I have learned that unless something *feels* right, unless it falls in line with my own morals and values, it will not work for me. Outside forces can help guide you in the right direction, but they cannot make decisions for you. Only you can do that. Only you can hold on to your power or take it back.

> *Another world is not*
> *only possible; she is on*
> *her way. On a quiet day,*
> *I can hear her breathing.*
> —ARUNDHATI ROY, INDIAN ACTIVIST AND AUTHOR

7
WOMEN ON TOP:
HIGHLY SUCCESSFUL WOMEN BARE ALL

> Memories of our lives, of our work, and our deeds
> will continue in others.
> —**Rosa Parks**

Throughout the early research for my first book and, more recently, during my many seminars, I asked hundreds of women what, in particular, they would like to see included in a book about empowerment. Without fail, they all mentioned they wanted to hear from women who had overcome obstacles similar to the ones they themselves had faced. They also wanted successful women to share with them their wisdom and advise on how to become an empowered woman. I believe these five women fill the bill. Their personal stories as well as their knowledge and hard-earned expertise will certainly inspire you to take back your power.

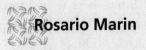 **Rosario Marin**

Forty-first treasurer of the United States; 2004 U.S. Senate candidate

After President George W. Bush named Rosario Marin the treasurer of the United States in 2001, she addressed the Senate this way: "When I came from Mexico at age fourteen, I did not speak English. I was frightened." No one would ever have guessed that this icon of female empowerment had been forced to overcome so many seemingly insurmountable obstacles. But in fact, the once frightened little girl who knew no English had an irrepressible spirit. She had set her mind to reaching her dreams from the get-go, never taking no for an answer, and she had succeeded against all odds.

After graduating from Harvard University and spending several years working in the private sector, Marin realized that she would need to work in a career that satisfied her profound need to give back to the community. She was elected to the Huntington Park City Council in 1994 and overwhelmingly reelected in 1999, before serving as mayor of the same city—which is near Los Angeles and has eighty-five thousand residents. After being appointed treasurer of the United States—she is the first Latina to reach such a prestigious position in the federal government—Marin beamed to a crowd and exclaimed, "Only in America."

Marin has absolutely embraced the tenets of living an empowered life. She also continues to keep it real. "I'm definitely afraid. I just do it!" Marin said recently. "There is never the perfect time to run for the United States Senate, to have a baby, or to get married, but there is an appropriate time. My grandmother always told me, *El que no se arriesga, no gana* [Nothing risked, nothing gained]. You need to take measurable risks in life to win."

Marin's story is one of struggles—struggles she overcame through determination, staying true to her beliefs, and believing in herself—but she does not dwell on the difficult times. She has made it as far as she has through perseverance, self-respect, faith, courage, and informed risk taking. She's had her fair share of critics, of people questioning her worth. "I was confronted with situations many times in many different ways. You have to make a conscious decision [about] what you are doing, and you have to be willing to lose in order to claim your self-respect. If you do that, you never really lose. You stand up for what you believe in. I have a lot of faith. I believe strongly that things happen for a reason. I believe that we are all here for a purpose. When I stand up for what I believe in, whether in politics or anything else, I am not only standing up for myself, but for people like me. It's not just for my family or my community—it is for families and communities like mine. Our lives are so much bigger than ourselves."

Marin also has a special devotion to people with disabilities, a commitment that earned her the distinguished Rose Fitzgerald Kennedy Prize at the United Nations in 1995. The award, which is considered the highest international recognition, had been given only one time before. "When I had my son Eric, who was born with Downs syndrome, I was twenty-seven and beginning my life in politics. If I took Eric with me to a political event, people would make comments that I wanted the 'pity vote.' If I didn't take him, people would comment that I was ashamed of him. Either way, I could not win. This was the defining moment for me. I decided then that I was not going to make decisions [based] on what other people thought of me. I was going to make all of my decisions [according to] what I thought was right. I care very little about what people think of me! I do seek advice from others, but people will always have conflicting opinions. I listen to the advice, but at the end of the day, I make my own decisions. It's very liberating to do what you think is best. I truly believe that we are all bigger than our challenges. Everything we go through is preparing us for the true tests of life."

Above all, Marin believes in herself. She is unstoppable because she trusts her inner voice, her higher power, her own intelligence, and her individuality. "Self-respect is having a sense of what you believe and standing with conviction for it. You have to be true to yourself and what you believe in. If you cannot be true to yourself, you cannot ask that anyone else be true to themselves. You cannot ask for something [that] you are not willing to offer. You cannot expect anyone to respect you unless you respect yourself first. I will *never* compromise my self-respect. Integrity is much easier kept than recovered. At the end of the day, all you have is yourself. You have to be able to look at yourself in the mirror every day and know that you did not have to give up yourself to do the right thing. There is a line you never cross."

Living a successful life was never in question for Marin. Her ability to develop her own strong set of personal beliefs enabled her to set out on her path early on. The respect she has earned from some of the most powerful people in the world is testament to the respect she has for herself. The rules are simple: self-respect breeds confidence, confidence breeds success, and success breeds respect from outside. This is true regardless of one's station in life. If a woman chooses to be a housewife, she should be a self-respecting wife and mother; if a woman chooses to be a politician, she should never compromise herself. "Always do the right thing, even if no one will ever find out; always give your best, even if you can get away with giving less; and always treat everybody with respect. That's what I tell my children."

Claudia Trejos

First Latina sports anchor in the United States

Claudia Trejos has been a source of controversy since her debut as a Los Angeles sports anchor in 1999. Criticized, and even ridiculed, in some of the country's major newspapers for what commentators perceived as inexperience and lack of knowledge in a variety of sports, she has had to fight an uphill battle despite her professionalism, knowledge, and presentation skills. She is a fighter, though. "Hell will freeze over before I let them win," she said at the time. Trejos is an irrepressible spirit, and her story is an inspiration to women everywhere. I recently talked with her about her life challenges and the principles she lives by.

Claudia, tell me about your family background.

I'm mixed racially. My dad's family is Turkish. My mom, she's also mixed, but she's basically Colombian—Indian Colombian—and there's some Italian in there somewhere. She's definitely a mestiza.

You're such a courageous person. Do you think you were born with that courage, or did you learn it? Did it just come naturally?

It's a combination. But I think it's in the blood. My dad never finished grammar school, and I already talked to you about my mom a little bit. It's genetically engraved in my body. I think life throws you curveballs that teach you how to deal with stuff. And you learn how to just get ahold of the bull by the horns.

But is that by taking risks, or doing what? A lot of women get thrown a lot of stuff, and they just seem to stay down.

It's a choice you make. The problem with women who might just choose to stay down is that they may be comfortable being down. See, I'm not comfortable being down. I would never take courage from people who decide, "This is what I want, and this is what I'm going to hold on to, even if my life is imperiled." I was not comfortable with not trying. I'd rather find out if I could than always wonder.

And that's something that you feel is in your blood? You never really learned that?

Not really, I don't think. From a very young age, I was questioning, always, how far I could go, and I was always pushing the envelope and allowing myself to explore. Interestingly enough, I was a very shy, quiet little girl. Throughout grammar school, I was very introverted because I was dyslexic, and had a lot of issues with learning. I tackled reading on a teleprompter; I enjoyed it because I couldn't do it before.

So you like challenges?

Yes. When I was five years old, they told my dad I was never going to learn how to read. At the time, they didn't know what dyslexia was. My dad said, "She's not stupid, so she's going to stay in a private bilingual school until I say she's not going to go." Not only did I learn how to read and write, but I learned how to read and write in two different languages. I've been speaking English since I was four.

The big challenges when I was little were with my parents. When my mom or dad said no to me about something, I had to find out why. They had to give me a good enough reason why, and if it wasn't valid for me, I would question the fallacy of their statements and then call them on it.

And you were allowed to do that? Wasn't it a sign of disrespect?

I was not allowed to do that. I got my butt kicked many times. And finally, you learn how to pick your fights, because it would have been hell for me. And I've got to say, there were times when I realized, as I got older, [that I wasn't] fighting the right battles. So I learned how to choose my fights and be very obser- vant, and then I realized that it was a lot easier to say "I'm sorry" than to ask for permission. I think one of the issues that made me become who I am today is the fact that my dad always expected the best of me.

But the best for him—was that the best for you, too, given that he was a traditional male as far as women are concerned? Wouldn't the best for you be sub- servience to your man?

No, which was a dichotomy in his lifestyle. When we have conversations now, he says, "I was preparing you for a different era, because the world that I was living in was not what you were going to inherit." Yes, and he also realized that he could only hold on to me for so long, especially with my character. He knew that if he hung on, if he held on too tight, I was going to slip away. I was always very inquisitive. He knew that my curiosity was going to take me very, very far.

So how do you feel about being the first Latina sports anchor in America?

That sounds like a lot, but it is only a job. You can't get caught up in it. You can't let anything get to you, either good or bad. What happens is that you lose perspective about where you are coming from and where you are going. I mean, I've lived in my car before.

You have shown an incredible amount of courage by standing up and not giving in to criticism. The old-boy network can bring anybody down.

Oh, yeah! It can, and they would if you allowed them to. It's a losing battle. What it really comes down to is . . . well, if I were an Anglo anchor, my critics wouldn't have a problem. And you know what? If you look across the table, everybody has an accent in their own way. They don't only have a problem with me because of my Hispanic accent but because, all of a sudden, there's a five-foot-two, one-hundred-twenty-pound female Hispanic sports anchor. Then it becomes a big deal.

How did you deal with the harsh criticism?

At first I had that feeling of What's going on here? Then, all of a sudden, it made sense. I realized that's why they're doing this. That's how it felt. You see, the criticism when I started was not the beginning. It became public when I started here, but it started six months before, when I was at Channel 22.

The *Los Angeles Times* was writing about me, and I didn't know why. It was like, "All she knows about is soccer and boxing." What they didn't realize is that I had been at a Hispanic station, where soccer and boxing were our bread and butter. The Dodgers were not the priority. If I had time, I would put in a piece on the Dodgers if they had a big win or if they had a tremendous loss to some weaker team or something major. When I got the offer from KTLA, I was thinking, well, I had the number one sports-magazine show in Los Angeles, and I was having fun—because that's how I ended up doing sports, because I enjoy it. Besides, it was an offer that I could not refuse. So when I started here and the criticism got worse, then I understood—I'm a threat. I was a threat when I was at Channel 22, and I'm a threat now that I'm at KTLA. I'm the one person they do not know. I came out of left field, and they had no idea what to expect from me; so basically, for six months I endured the worst criticism because they didn't know me. After that, it was only for about three or four months that they kept writing and talking about me on air. But it was like those new pair of shoes that you love, and you know they look good, but they hurt like crazy. And you got to wear 'em and wear 'em until they finally contour to your foot. That's how it felt.

How do you feel about compromise?

I don't think I have to compromise. But it's an issue, because life is about compromises. You don't have everything; you can't have everything—there's no way on earth. The more rational side of me says there's no way I'm going to have everything I've ever wanted. So somewhere along the line, I have to compromise. But the little girl in me says, "I'm not giving jack!" Because this is mine, you know what I'm saying?

Do you live by many cultural traditions?

Yes and no. I guess I take what works for me.

How do you feel about your culture's definition of respect? Do you believe that young women should respect their elders, even when the elders don't respect them?

Hmmm, that's a huge issue. Now, if you respect your elders—and those role models are disrespectful of you—that could create low self-esteem and all the terrible things that come with that. That's a very, very interesting question. If you have a sixteen- or seventeen-year-old who is assertive, most likely she will say something to her elders if disrespected. But if you tell somebody at five or six that she's stupid, or underestimate her abilities or her future, the problem becomes that at sixteen or seventeen, she's going to take that [attitude] from everybody. The problem lies in lack of education. Those elders are very uneducated, and they come from a country where to be subservient was the only way to survive. Many were married off by the time they were thirteen, fourteen, to whoever would take them, in order to be fed and have a roof over their heads. That was the only way their parents could assure their daughters or granddaughters that they were going to have a safe future.

Why do you think a vast number of young Latinas are suffering from low self-esteem and depression?

Because we have been conditioned to be crowd pleasers. Our culture has confusing messages. We're expected to be sluts in bed, but we're expected to be virgins when we get married. We're expected to be chefs in the kitchen and assertive in the workforce. Perfect Mother Teresas! There are only so many things we can conquer at one time. And then we have the grandma that wants us to pray a gazillion Hail Marys before we go to bed, and we have the boyfriends who want us to give it up; but if we give it up, then they won't marry us. What the hell is wrong with us? And then our dads are sending us to school to be independent, yet they are keeping our mothers in virtual domestic slavery. Talk about dichotomies!

What would you tell women who feel they have no support when they do something positive for themselves? What would be your message to them?

To believe in themselves, because eventually, the only person who will carry you through everything will be you. Yeah, you're going to have people cheering, but they're just cheering. Those cheers, as we know in the NFL, don't make players win games. And it's hard. At no point in time would I ever say it's easy. And that's why it's so important for us to find out what we want to do in life, where we want to see ourselves in x number of years. The last thing I would like to say is that we all have courage; we need to use our courage to live the life we want and to carry us through the hard times. We will never know that courage until we call on it and use it.

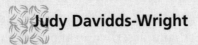 Judy Davidds-Wright

Certified corporate-etiquette and international protocol consultant, and CEO of Distinguished Professionals, a company that provides group training and personal coaching on business, social, and dining etiquette

Judy Davidds-Wright has secured a reputation as a pioneering, powerful, and dedicated leader during her sixteen-year career working in the corporate and public sectors. She has worked closely with clients ranging from young professionals to seasoned, top-tier executives. She has built strong relationships with some of the world's largest and most successful Hispanic organizations, media representatives, politicians, and business and community leaders. Davidds-Wright has raised the bar of business and social-etiquette education by combining her background in the corporate and public sectors with her intimate understanding of people. Here, she shares her views on the role of proper behavior in the workplace.

How to Gain Respect in the Corporate World with Class

Whether you're an executive, manager, saleswoman, administrative assistant, customer-service representative, or recent college graduate—or you're reentering the workforce after electing to raise children full-time—you can gain a sense of empowerment, and greater success in the corporate arena, by knowing how to use etiquette to your advantage. Attire and grooming are obvious, but there are other, often overlooked, details that play a major role. Your body language projects a professional, confident presence, and your professional behavior helps you command respect. The key is that gender does not play a role in business etiquette. Yes, you can and should hold the door, stand when greeting someone, and pay the bill when hosting a meal, regardless of whether you are dealing with a man or woman. Subconsciously, this communicates that you are equal and deserve equal respect.

No, ladies, I'm not saying it's time to toss the stiletto pumps that gained you access to the most happening event in town. Nor should you stop dressing sexy for your man. There is a time and a place for such activities, and work is not it. What I am saying is, stop giving weak handshakes, batting your eyelashes, tossing your hair, and expecting special treatment because you're a woman. If you do this to a man, he'll think you're easy and won't take you and your work seriously. If you do it to a woman, she'll think you're flaky and won't take you and your work seriously. If you want to change the way others respond to you, you must change your actions. Examine your behavior and attitudes honestly. We've all been conditioned to act a certain way according to our cultural influences. This behavior, however, will not always work in the corporate world. Adopt the protocol of the company you work for, but never compromise your integrity.

Fresh out of college, I worked for a very conservative top Fortune 100 company. Nylons and closed-toe pumps were a must. Whether or not I believed this to be appropriate was irrelevant. I accepted the job knowing the rules, and it was my responsibility to respect company protocol. I loved my job and my boss. However, that all changed when a female manager joined the department. It was evident that I was not one of her favorite people. Did I mention she was best friends with the CEO? Many times I felt that she was sabotaging me. On several occasions she accused me of disregarding her instructions and intentionally proceeding with the project my way. Then she would have me start all over again and discreetly share with the others that the setback was because of me. Being young, inexperienced, and in dire need of a job—and having been taught to respect my elders and those in a higher position, no matter what— I chose to remain silent. I could easily have badmouthed the manager, but I didn't. My peers had no power to change the situation, and besides, I had no proof of my boss's sabotage. I started dreading going to work and became emotionally exhausted.

Finally, one day she slipped and her manipulations became evident. I was able to confirm with a vendor an initial request that she had later changed and blamed me for not following through. I approached her with caution, choosing my words carefully. Even when confronted with the evidence, however, she denied everything. At that moment, I could have chosen to explode emotionally or bring the matter to the CEO. I choose the latter. I walked into his office and closed the door. I shared all that I had been experiencing, hoping for some type of relief. I could see empathy in his eyes as I explained the situation. However, he offered no solution because of his personal relationship with the manager. I thanked him for his time and told him that I understood his position, but I also understood that it was time for me to leave.

There comes a time when you must speak up—not aggressively or emotionally or by whining, but firmly and clearly. In order to change others' perceptions of you, and their behavior toward you, you must first learn to respect yourself. The alternative is to condemn yourself to an unhealthy work environment.

Remember: etiquette is power!

Carrie Lopez

Executive director, Coro Southern California

Before Carrie Lopez joined Coro, a leadership-development organization in Southern California, she was a community-relations manager with a private firm in San Diego. She gained extensive government experience while serving with the city of San Diego, the office of California state senator Nicholas Petris, and the office of U.S. senator Alan Cranston. As a member of the San Luis Rey Mission Indians, Lopez is a special adviser to the tribal council on federal government issues. Currently, she is the chair of the

HOPE Leadership Institute, an organization she co-founded, dedicated to influencing policy issues and the political process throughout California. She also serves on advisory committees for several local organizations, including the Los Angeles Department of Neighborhood Empowerment. Lopez holds a bachelor's degree in international relations and world politics from the University of California, Davis, and a master's degree in public administration from the Kennedy School of Government at Harvard University. Lopez completed the California Senate Fellows Program and the Leadership America Program.

In the following essay, Lopez points out the role of selfless vision in achieving the kind of success that is meaningful and everlasting.

It's Not All About You

How do you invest your talents, passion, and energy into a pursuit while ensuring that its success continues beyond you? The answer: by creating a legacy, not a dynasty.

What is the difference? A dynasty is about you. A legacy is about others. If you are creating something that is wonderful but primarily dependent on you, and your identity is wrapped up in its success, then you are developing a dynasty. A dynasty is created almost entirely through your effort and primarily for your success. It will continue and thrive as long as you are in control. But dynasties come and go. Legacies endure beyond your individual effort.

When do you know you are creating a legacy? It starts with your intentions in the beginning, your ambitions connected to the project, and your deliberate actions to connect your vision to the visions of others. A legacy is not a short-term project; it's more purposeful. A legacy results from a great idea that is inspired, molded, and cultivated by individuals committed to a common mission.

Before we start singing "Kumbaya," let me clarify a couple of things. Building a legacy requires ambition, a healthy ego, and leadership. A legacy requires you to contribute your time and talent to something larger than yourself. In essence, a legacy includes you but is not about you.

Let's say it together: "When I am invested in ensuring a legacy, I need to accept that it is not about me in the end. I can be the inspiration; I can be the motivator; I can provide the talent, energy, persistence, time, and personality. But from beginning to end, my guiding principle must result in something more than a platform for my increased recognition, or a home for my identity."

Legacies are a tough prospect and are not meant to be easy. When you invest your time and emotion in anything, it starts to feel like a part of you. It's instinctual. But it's also a combination of some sense of responsibility, a desire for success, and a fear of failure or embarrassment, with a dash of control freak. Don't misunderstand me—your investment has to be worth your time. But your self-interest cannot be the sole guiding principle of a potential legacy.

There is always a moment when you have to set in motion a potential legacy versus a dynasty. My moment came several years ago when I was working on a leadership project for an organization called HOPE.

HOPE is one of a few organizations that are devoted to the advancement of Latinas in California. The group isn't any more special, qualified, or important than the others, but it had a great idea and an ace in the hole. The idea was to run a leadership-training program for Latinas who wanted to be more savvy about politics. The theory was that economic, civic, and political power all fed one another. The ace was a board president who had developed the critical relationships with organizations and companies that were ready to invest in Latinas for this purpose. And they had one more asset: me. I would end up nurturing a great idea into a powerful accomplishment.

I fell into a wonderful opportunity that combined my love of politics, my talent as a trainer, and my desire to make a difference in larger communities through the empowerment of Latina leaders. In my mind, this was the chance to be part of a larger legacy. And though I knew I would be a vital part of it, I also needed to pull out the reality checklist. Who was the project for? What would make it a success at the start? What would make it a success in five or ten years? What would that success look like? How could I ensure that it would be successful without me in the driver's seat?

The danger was that it was also the perfect pedestal for someone like me. I could design the program to promote my politics. The women who decided to run for office could feel beholden to me for their success. I could be promoted as the perfect Latina leader whom everyone should try to emulate. I could break the project away from HOPE. But once I faced what success would look like for this project, the plan was clear: to create a network of Latinas throughout the state who felt empowered to improve their communities through their individual and collective efforts. My dynasty would not accomplish this—it would be a disaster because it was focused on me. It had to include more talents than my own; more people had to feel responsible for it than just me; and I, alone, could not facilitate all of the connections and promotion of the women involved.

What helped keep me on track was my own habit of

continually putting myself in others' shoes. The participants and alumnae had to believe in the sincerity of the project. They were investing their precious time throughout the year to a cause that was larger than themselves, and they needed to be convinced that I was making an equal commitment. The sponsors of the project had to trust the integrity of our effort, too. They needed the assurance that we were investing in women who were dedicated to their communities and not beholden to one agenda over another. And most important, this was a public project. This was not my personal business in which I was in charge, making the decisions, making the money, making a profit, and paying the taxes. No, this project was offered to the public by a public, nonprofit corporation, for a public benefit. Translation: the women of HOPE had to own this project in every way. They had to understand it, shape its future, invest in relationships with the participants and graduates, feel responsible for its success, and enjoy the success.

I said earlier that there is a moment when you set a legacy in motion. That's true. But the reinforcement of that decision and commitment takes much longer. My commitment to myself was to invest in something great without sacrificing what was great about me. In other words, I couldn't put all of myself in this effort, because there was a lot more to me than that. This project could not end up defining me. I would not let myself be limited. And the more I focused my energies on ensuring the legacy, the more I was able to see it come to life. I have no doubt that I have a crucial role, no doubt that my spirit is embedded in what the women are committed to, and no doubt that when the program ends, we will all look back and say, "I was part of something important; we all made it happen; and the world is a little better because of it."

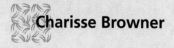
Charisse Browner

President and executive director of radio station
Power 106 FM's nonprofit fund Knowledge Is Power and
host of the weekly program by the same name

Born in a poor area of San Diego, Browner overcame the damage of years of sexual abuse during her
childhood and an abusive marriage to become a powerhouse of change. She began her career at Power 106 FM
a decade ago and has since become the station's eyes and
ears in the community. "Everyone in the community
should have a voice, have an outlet in which to be heard
or to find answers to their questions. Helping people is
so natural to me. Being able to educate our listeners is
what it's all about." The Knowledge Is Power Foundation's overall mission is to help develop skills and self-
empowerment by way of on-the-job training opportunities
and educational programs for at-risk youth from East
and South Central Los Angeles. Since its inception, the
foundation has raised $2.7 million for schools and com-
munity projects.

In a conversation with me, Browner, who lives in Los
Angeles with her two teenage children, shared the
tragedies she faced at various points in her life and how,
eventually, she took back her power.

Tell me how you saw your world growing up.

My world felt like it was black and white. I grew up
in Logan Heights, a poor area of San Diego. All
blacks lived in poor areas, and whites lived somewhere else. The issue of ethnicity was never brought

up in our household . . . all I knew is that no whites lived in our area. They were a whole world apart.

How did you see your place in the world?

I grew up with two different kinds of youths. One was fun . . . there were many kids in my extended family so we would always be playing outside, climbing on fences, building mud pies, and having a blast. My second one was something that no child would want to endure . . . molestation. This life was dark and empty and it caused me to be very self-destructive.

At what age did the molestation start?

I think it was probably when I was a baby because my mother worked three jobs so she would leave us, my brothers, sister, and I, with my grandparents [her parents]. My grandpa was my king; I felt he loved me and I adored him. But he was also my molester. The first memory I have of my grandfather molesting me was when I was four years old.

Didn't your grandmother know what was going on?

I am pretty sure she knew because there were times I would sleep in the middle of her and my grandfather in their bed and he would sexually abuse me. People don't think it is possible for abuse to take place if there is a third person in the same bed, but that is wrong, because it happened to me. Yet she believed my grandfather was the head of the household and feared him. My grandmother depended on him financially and believed she would not be able to make it without him, so she just pretended it wasn't happening.

How did you deal with the molestation as a child?

I created a separate identity; there were two of me. One was nice and sweet, which is the one I showed to my grandfather because I loved him so much. The other was mean and cruel; so mean that if someone said something I didn't like, I would spit on them. I didn't like being a mean child but I guess that's how my anger manifested itself.

Did you tell anyone this was happening to you?

The abuse stopped when I was twelve years old. I just refused to continue going to my grandfather's house. I didn't tell anyone about it until my twenty-first birthday, when I told my mother. The first words that came out of my mother's mouth were, "I thought I was the only one."

If your mother had been abused by her father, why did she let him take care of you?

That was the biggest issue I had with my mother until the day she died. I would ask her why she left me with him after he had abused her and she would tell me, "I don't know." That answer was never good enough for me. It took me twenty years to finally forgive her—she was on her deathbed.

What made you forgive her? How did you come to terms with this?

On June 16, 2004, my mother was on her deathbed at the hospital, dying of multiple myeloma, a cancer of the blood. She was in a lot of pain and suffering on a daily basis. I was in the hospital's lobby reading the newspaper when a pamphlet about death fell out of the paper. I began to read. It said, "If the body shuts down and it takes a little longer for the person to pass away, it is because the spirit was holding on . . . it has unfinished business." My mother's body had shut down and she was ready to pass away, yet I felt it was her spirit that needed to hear me say I forgave her for not protecting me from my grandfather. I went to her side and whispered in her ear, "Mom, I love you and I forgive you." She died the next day.

Did your mother ever confront her father about the abuse?

Yes, and of course he denied it at first. Later he told her that it wasn't a big deal. That she did not need to make a fuss about it. After that, my mother was never the same again; she became a sad person. It interfered with her relationships with men; she didn't trust them and taught me that all men are worthless cheats.

How did all of this impact you?

As a young adult, from about age fourteen to twenty-six, I didn't trust people, I was always suspicious of them and I believed men only wanted one thing. I believed my worth was between my legs. During those years I looked really good. I was a model, so many people would compliment me and tell me how beautiful I was. I would respond negatively to their comments and people thought I was conceited. In reality, I felt ugly inside.

When did things start to change for you?

I got married to a famous NFL player who was very abusive, would cheat on me and tell me I was worthless. When I told him that my grandfather molested me, he responded with, "Oh your grandpa tapped that ass before I did." That's when my marriage went down the drain. I realized I needed to take care of myself because no one else was going to do it.

Were there times in your life when you felt you gave your power away?

Absolutely. All through my teens and twenties I was a doormat, a puppet. I really felt I had no power. All this was the result of the molestation. Although I knew I was smart, it seemed like it really didn't matter because my worth was between my legs anyway. I really gave my power away to my husband. Throughout our marriage I felt powerless; at times he would tell me when I could or could not speak. The more I stayed in that marriage, the more powerless I felt.

How did you begin to reclaim your power?

One night I was at my wit's end. I couldn't take it anymore and I prayed to God, asking him to please show me what I needed to do to get out of this horrible life I was living. When I woke up the next morning, I went straight to the hair salon and cut off my beautiful long hair. I felt sooooo powerful. I don't know what it was but I woke up that morning with a sense of strength and power I had never felt before. Cutting my hair signified freedom for me because when I was little my grandfather never let me cut my hair. He loved my beautiful long hair and would tell me that my hair was for him. He would get angry if he saw my hair down while I talked to boys because he said my hair was only for his eyes. I truly believe it was God who gave me the strength to break free. I took my two kids and left my husband. Although we had to go on welfare at that time, I was happy because I was free!

Did reclaiming your power help you heal your wounds?

Absolutely! I have come such a long way and I love where I am at right now. I spent a lot of time alone with myself taking care of me. I realized I had to turn myself around and I did. I am so strong now.

Do your life experiences have anything to do with your career choice?

Yes. I always had compassion for people and wanted to help people. I was the one who always volunteered to do things that would help people. Becoming the president of the Knowledge Is Power Foundation fulfilled a deep void within myself. In my radio show I cover many taboo topics and educate the community, so others don't have to go through what I went through.

8 FOLLOW THE YELLOW BRICK ROAD:
EXERCISES TO GET THERE FROM WHEREVER YOU ARE

I've a feeling we're not in Kansas anymore.
—Dorothy, in *The Wizard of Oz*

At this point, you've taken in a lot of information, much of which may be completely new to you. Change is never easy, but nothing worth so much *should* be easy. This book is meant to be read and reread again whenever you need inspiration, guidance, and affirmation that the decision to implement changes in your life is a positive one. I have included this chapter of exercises to help set you on your way, with the hope that the work you do here will serve as a launchpad for a lifetime of self-realization.

Please take your time and work through the following exercises at a pace that is comfortable for you. If certain exercises spark your imagination or provoke your thoughts, feel free to customize them for yourself. Not all of these exercises will directly apply to your unique circumstances, but because the ultimate goal is for you to control your own destiny, you should decide how to make the most of these tools. You can revisit these exercises whenever you like, as often as you like. You are an evolving being, and on your road to empowerment, you will find that your ideas about many things will change. Take your first step and embrace that change—it means that you are growing.

Step 1. Write Your Life Story

In Chapter One, I told you something about my life, from childhood through some very difficult years. I recounted some of my most devastating trials and how they affected my growth from a girl into a woman. When I was asked to write my life story for the first time, I had no idea how or where to begin. What would I include? What was significant enough to commit to writing?

Why was this an important therapeutic exercise? What I learned during the process was that, yes, I had a story of survival to share with the world, but I also had plenty of completely new realizations about who I am and how I came to be the woman I am. I learned that by looking back at my past from a new perspective and with kinder eyes, I could discover a whole new side of myself.

Think of life as a tapestry. By analyzing the people and events that have influenced you in both negative and positive ways, you can pick out patterns that will profoundly affect the process of self-discovery. As you recall people, events, and emotions from your past, you begin to "own" your unique history; you acknowledge your own mistakes, as well as the mistakes of others, and you forgive, thereby relieving yourself of a burden that's probably holding you back from being truly empowered. Once you can own both your successes and mistakes, your self-awareness and confidence will grow tenfold and you will find the freedom to love the person you were born to be. When you truly know yourself, you can finally acknowledge and embrace your inherent power.

Writing your life story shouldn't be like a homework assignment or a task you'd rather put off. It doesn't have to be structured chronologically, and it doesn't even have to be grammatically correct. You're not going for a work of literature here, you're doing this for yourself. Be aware of sugarcoating events or behaviors. In order to learn something, you must be completely honest—remember, you don't have to share your work with anyone. It can require days or even weeks to recall all of the significant experiences in your life—it is an ongoing process—and you should try to approach it as something enjoyable. The steps outlined below are meant to be carried out over a fairly lengthy period of time, but it's important not to let the process go on indefinitely. At this point, it is most important to just begin.

1. Find a quiet, comfortable spot where you can concentrate for at least an hour at a time. The method you use—whether it be longhand, typing on the computer, or even speaking into a tape recorder—doesn't matter so much as your comfort level. Clear extraneous thoughts from your head. If you are hungry or if you are expecting an important phone call, you won't be able to give this exercise the proper focus.

2. Begin by thinking about an exceptional experience from your past. This may be something that happened dur-

ing childhood, or something that happened more recently. What is most important is that this event somehow impacted you in a significant way. There are certainly numerous events and people who have shaped who you are, but to begin, choose just one. Close your eyes, go back in time, and try to relive the circumstances leading up to that experience. For now, simply describe in a few sentences what happened, who you were with, how you felt physically and emotionally, and what ultimate effect the experience had on you.

3. Now consider the event in retrospect. Look back on the situation and write about why it was meaningful to you. What makes this experience important to write about? How does this particular experience factor in your life today?

4. Now you are ready to catalog other major events in your life. Often, events that make you feel uncomfortable provide for the most meaningful realizations. Instead of ignoring or refusing to acknowledge certain events, trust the process and allow yourself to feel. When you write, you can rest assured that your thoughts are private, but they are worthy. These events may be things that you spend a great deal of time and mental energy thinking about, but not necessarily acting on, or they may be things that you have repressed. This exercise is a perfect opportunity to release all of the anxiety those events have been causing you.

5. Let it all out. Open the floodgates and allow yourself to free your mind of the frustration you've kept bottled up inside. The act of writing or saying words without restriction is a huge step toward accepting the truth of what has influenced you. With acceptance comes the desire to make changes for the better so that you can claim owner-

ship over your past, your present, and your future. Write as much as you feel comfortable writing.

6. Relax and take a few minutes to review what you have written. Add any additional detail, insights, or meaning that may come to mind. Try to relive those experiences again, and make the decision to understand why those particular experiences stand out for you. What is your intuition trying to tell you?

7. Take a break and congratulate yourself. You have begun to acknowledge your own story. It's most important now to pay particular attention to dreams, coincidences, and intuitive hunches.

8. When you are ready, resume the writing process, adding to your narrative as you gain new insight. Anything and everything is pertinent at this point. Write all of your thoughts down, savor them, and try to understand the larger message.

9. After several days, during a quiet time, review all that you have written. Pay special attention to the similarities and the connections, but also to the contrasts.

Over the days, weeks, months, and years to come, put your story aside for a while every now and then, and then come back to it again. Additional insights and new experiences will always come to you, and by writing about them, you can more easily understand the impact they have on your life. In this ongoing process of learning about yourself, you will discover your deeper nature, your purpose, your connections, and you'll take ownership of your life story.

Step 2. Find Out Who's in Control

In Chapter Two, we discussed the myriad ways we give our power away. Our family members, our church, our communities, and our schools can influence us in ways we aren't even aware of until we're forced to acknowledge them. Until we reach that point, we are still living under someone—or something—else's control because we are viewing ourselves through outside forces. The following exercises can help you determine if you are really in control of your own life.

Think carefully, and answer each question honestly.

- Do you always follow the rules?
- Do you ever question the sensibleness of rules?
- Is being viewed as obedient important to you?
- Do you feel guilty deviating from the rules?
- Do you find yourself engaging in soothing behavior when conflict arises?
- Are you unable to communicate your own frustrations or upset feelings directly?
- Do you feel you need to be in a romantic relationship to feel safe and secure?
- Do you have a low tolerance to being alone and enjoying your own company?
- Does having total financial and emotional responsibility for yourself frighten you?
- Do you feel you are *not* living your life to the fullest?
- Will you often do things you don't want to do in order to avoid disapproval?

- Do people's opinions about you concern you?
- Do you have difficulty saying "no"?
- Is it very important that you do not disappoint others?
- Do you feel guilty when you disappoint someone?
- Are you persuaded easily?
- In a professional situation, do you have difficulty speaking out?
- Is it ever difficult for you to express a different point of view?
- Do you avoid being viewed as a wave maker?
- Do you see being a wave maker as being a troublemaker?

If you answered "yes" to several of these questions, you are probably allowing external factors to control your life (that is, allowing people, places, and things to determine your course for you). It is said that no man is free who is not master of himself—the same is absolutely true for women. Every woman ought to do with her life as she wishes. If you are surrounded by people who usurp your power and make your decisions for you, or if you make decisions based on a need for love and acceptance, you will never be free.

Step 3. Determine How Tight Are Your Family Ties

What do you believe? No, not those beliefs—not the ones you inherited! *Your* beliefs, the ones that are hidden deep down in your soul. The ones you had to tuck away due to your fear of disapproval. The checklist below will help you reach into your subconscious and determine your own real and true beliefs and identify your underlying feelings and behaviors. Put a mark next to each statement that you feel relates to you.

In my relationship with my parents and family, I believe . . .

__It is up to me to make my parents happy.

__It is up to me to make my parents proud.

__I am my parents' whole life.

__If I told my parents the truth about my divorce (my abortion, my being gay, my fiancé being an atheist . . .), it would kill them.

__If I stand up to my parents, they will be upset with me.

__If I tell my parents how much they have hurt me, they will cut me out of their lives.

__I shouldn't do or say anything that would hurt my parents' feelings.

__My parents' feelings are more important than mine.

__There's no point in talking to my parents because it would do no good.

__If my parents would only change, I would feel better about myself.

__If I could just get my family to see how much they are hurting me, I know they'd be different.

__No matter what they have done, they are my parents and I have to honor them.

__My parents don't have any control over my life; I fight with them all the time.

If four or more of these apply to you, you are giving your power away to your family and culture because of negative beliefs. Although we may not want to accept it, all of the beliefs listed above are self-defeating. They prevent us from owning our power, they increase dependency, and they rob us of something that is our birthright. In order to reclaim this power, we must admit that we are giving it away in the first place. When you can be honest enough to acknowledge that you are actively participating in your own manipulation (even if the intent is good), you can demonstrate to the world that you are ready to take the driver's seat on your own journey of life.

Step 4. Locate Yourself: South or North of the Border?

When you neglect to establish boundaries, you inevitably give your power away, whether in the home or out in the world. Respect is a natural consequence of other people abiding by your boundaries. This exercise will help you to recognize where you are lacking established boundaries, what the consequences are, and how you can change yourself (because you can't change anyone else). The numbered statements represent what happens when we lack healthy boundaries of our own creation. The questions posed will teach you to look to yourself for answers.

1. We are unable to defend ourselves when we are being disrespected or abused, whether emotionally, physically, or sexually.

When we grow up in a family with unhealthy (or non-existent) boundaries, we do not learn what is, and what is not, offensive and disrespectful behavior. Our emotions don't tell us to be offended, because we are out of touch with them. We are not aware that we are being disrespected because our definition of respect is distorted. Has anyone mistreated you or controlled you in ways you've felt were disrespectful? Why have you allowed the behavior to continue? Do you love yourself enough to defend yourself?

2. We give others too much power over our lives.

Does anyone have more power over you than they should? How have you given them that power? Why have you given them this power? What need of yours is being fulfilled by giving them this power?

3. We grow up without a sense of self.

Without boundaries, we get lost in the identity of someone else instead of embracing our own unique character. We allow someone else's attitudes and behaviors to dictate how we speak and behave and we deny ourselves the right to be our own person. We grow further and further away from our own feelings and preferences. What are some things that you have done, or now do, to be accepted, or to avoid rejection? Do you realize that in doing these things you are giving your power away?

4. We deny ourselves by pretending to agree when we disagree.

We conceal our true feelings; we go along with an activity that we really don't want to do, and we never state our preferences. If we do have a preference, we won't say what it is, even when asked. We go along with the crowd. Have you recently disagreed with someone but didn't express your own opinion? Why didn't you express your opinion? What would have made you feel more comfortable?

5. When involved in an intimate relationship, we lose who we are and become who our mate wants us to be in order to be loved.

Have you ever sacrificed a part of yourself in order to be accepted or loved? Have you ever accepted behavior from a man that you had previously promised yourself you never would?

These are just a few examples of what can happen when we lack personal boundaries. Now it's your turn. Write five more consequences that you have personally been affected by because of a lack of defining what is and what is not acceptable to you. After each consequence, take an active part in your own healing by questioning your own motives, as well as the motives of the person influencing you. Respect is your birthright—if someone is draining you of this essential life force, you must search for answers within yourself.

Step 5. Learn the Difference Between "Want" and "Need"

The exercise below is intended to help you to set boundaries for an intimate relationship. List the appropriate items for each category as honestly as you can.

1. *My Needs in a Mate.* The things you *must* have in a mate, no matter what. Examples: honesty, communication (or willingness to learn how to communicate), trustworthiness, intelligence.
2. *My Wants in a Mate.* The things you would like but can live without. Examples: spirituality, a professional career, enjoyment of the same music.
3. *What I Will Not Accept from a Mate.* Examples: disrespect, cheating, violence.
4. *What I Am Willing to Give.* Examples: honesty, affection, commitment.
5. *What I Am Not Willing to Give Up.* Examples: time with friends, career, education.

Usually, the "My Needs" list and the "What I Am Willing to Give" list coincide with each other. Be careful not to ask for something you are not willing to offer, and remember that your mate should not ask you for something he is not willing to offer you, either.

Once we have set our boundaries, we must abide by them. Warning: people will test our limits in order to see how serious we are. Adhering to newly established positions is a difficult task, particularly for women who have held on to feelings of guilt and shame. It is terribly important to release this guilt. Out of fear of being alone, many women stay in harmful relationships. In order to combat this fear, we must be truthful with ourselves and open up to those who will support us. We need to expose ourselves to new teachings and information in order to overcome the negative images embedded in our culture in regard to our sexuality. We need to build a network of support, and realize that we are not alone in the fight against the old messages and the guilt involved during the process of change.

I encourage all women to set their own individual, healthy boundaries, and to find the courage to abide by them. We cannot change how others think, nor can we control their reactions to our new set of individual limits. This holds true whether we are talking about sexuality, respect, faith, cultural influences, or anything else that contributes to our process of self-empowerment. The exercises found in this chapter can guide you and help you to identify the root causes of what might be holding you back from being the whole person you are meant to be. It's important to keep in mind that all the answers can be found within yourself; you are your own best source of information.

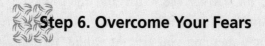 Step 6. Overcome Your Fears

I define "fear" as False Evidence Appearing Real. Fear-based belief systems are created from negative messages that are out of alignment with the truth, yet we accept them almost mindlessly. We need to identify which false beliefs are creating fear and causing us to give up our power so that we can replace them with the truth, thereby regaining our power. A very important step in that process is to recognize and acknowledge your achievements, and to analyze your successes.

List four things that you are proud of achieving.

1. _____

2. _____

3. _____

4. _____

Describe what led up to each of those achievements. Here are some things to consider:

• Were you scared or anxious at any point on the path to your success?
• How did you overcome that fear?
• Did your beliefs about what you can handle change after you reached your success?
• What qualities do you feel you developed in the process of these successes?
• How can you apply what you have learned toward something that you have been fearing?

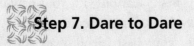 ## Step 7. Dare to Dare

This exercise will help you determine how comfortable you are with taking chances.

1. You're at a dinner party with people you don't know well. The conversation is dragging, and you remember a hilarious joke that a friend recently told you. You
   a. _____ tell the joke, of course.
   b. _____ quietly tell the joke to the woman sitting next to you (if she thinks it's funny, then you'll repeat it to rest of the group).
   c. _____ would feel uncomfortable telling a joke at a dinner party.

2. You're picnicking at a lake where some teenagers are jumping off a high rock into the water below. Some-

one in your group tries to rally everyone to take the plunge. You

a. _____ hang out in the wading area.

b. _____ watch the others do it for a while and then jump.

c. _____ are the first one to join the kids.

3. Your boss calls you into her office and informs you that you're fired. You

a. _____ press her for details on exactly went wrong.

b. _____ panic and beg her to give you another chance.

c. _____ are shocked initially, but find yourself dreaming of new opportunities as security escorts you out the door.

4. You are going on your first vacation with your new man, who is sweet but very proper and conservative. As a bon voyage present, your best friend gives you some very sexy lingerie. You

a. _____ hide it in your bottom drawer (maybe you'll wear it on your honeymoon).

b. _____ wear it proudly on the first night of your trip.

c. _____ flip through a Victoria's Secret catalog in front of him so you can gauge his reaction.

5. On Saturday night, you're most likely to be eating dinner

a. _____ at the West African place that opened up last week.

b. _____ at home, enjoying your trusty, tried-and-true pot roast.

c. _____ at your favorite little Italian café.

6. You're in a work meeting when you hear a superior

discussing a strategy that you think is off the mark.
You

a. ____ keep quiet—contradicting a superior is career
suicide.

b. ____ compliment something about the proposal,
and then suggest a variation.

c. ____ stay quiet for now, then go back to your
desk, research an alternate strategy, and present it to
your superior in private.

7. Your idea of adventure travel is

    a. ____ staying in a hotel rated with anything less
than five stars.

    b. ____ going on an African safari led by experienced
guides.

    c. ____ booking a cheap, last-minute flight to Nepal,
grabbing your backpack, and letting destiny take its
course.

8. You've spent half an hour flirting with a funny and dev-
astatingly handsome man at a party. When he looks at
his watch and announces that he's heading home, you

    a. ____ concoct some reason why you need to know
more about his business (you've always been fasci-
nated by commercial bank management, right?) and
offer to buy him a cup of coffee to "pick his brain."

    b. ____ wait until he leaves and then grill your host-
ess.

    c. ____ do nothing—if was into you, he wouldn't
have left.

9. You want to redecorate your home. You

    a. ____ replicate a room you found in a Pottery Barn
catalog, right down to the coasters.

    b. ____ opt for bold colors and adorn your home

with exotic trinkets found at street fairs, rummage sales, and antiques stores.

c. _____ consult magazines for inspiration but inject your own style by mixing and matching existing and new furnishings.

10. Your dinner parties

a. _____ meet all the dietary requirements of your guests; you always know who is vegetarian, who eats kosher, and who is allergic to shellfish.

b. _____ are usually thrown together at the last minute and feature whatever exotic cuisine you favor at the moment.

c. _____ You don't have dinner parties.

Score Yourself

1. a = 3, b = 2, c = 1
2. a = 1, b = 2, c = 3
3. a = 3, b = 2, c = 1
4. a = 1, b = 3, c = 2
5. a = 3, b = 1, c = 2
6. a = 1, b = 3, c = 2
7. a = 1, b = 2, c = 3
8. a = 3, b = 2, c = 1
9. a = 1, b = 2, c = 3
10. a = 2, b = 3, c = 1

If you scored between 1 and 10, you are the *Minimizer*

You're seduced by the rewards of the big risk, but you're not so keen on paying the price when it doesn't work out. To that end, you find different ways to lower the bar for yourself by perhaps applying for a less challenging job, or staying in a beginner dance class when you're really ready for intermediate. You also have a tendency to take "stealth" risks; for example, you may call someone you're romantically interested in under the pretense of business rather than being upfront about your intentions. In other words, you give yourself an out. This can work well for you, since you rarely speak out of turn, and many people find you to be extremely polite. But because you don't state your intentions directly, you frequently find that you're misunderstood, and that consequence can be worse than not taking a risk at all. To become a better risk taker, practice working without a net. Ask someone for a date, state your opinion outright, or try a new recipe out on your in-laws—anything that's a bit scary. You'll find that with greater risk comes a greater reward.

If you scored between 11 and 20, you are the *Information Gatherer*

You will take a risk, but only after carefully assessing all the pros and cons. Sometimes this works to your advantage—you've probably dodged some bad advice in your day. However, you've also let some great opportunities pass you by because you were so busy crunching numbers. To become a better risk taker, practice trusting your gut instinct on lower-stakes issues like selecting a birthday present or telling a joke. Then move on to big-ticket decisions like buying a home or confronting your fiancé about finally getting married. Obviously, you shouldn't stop doing your homework entirely, but you do need to accept that you can't anticipate every outcome, every time. At some point, you have to close your eyes and take the plunge.

If you scored between 21 and 30, you are the *High Roller*

Whether it's in the boardroom, the nightclub, or at the end of a bungee cord, you thrive on the adrenaline rush of taking big risks. Your natural resiliency and optimism let you shake off failures easily, and your sense of adventure means you rarely rest on your successes. You're always moving on to the next thing. You can, at times, be a bit too impulsive, rushing into the wrong job, relationship, or double-diamond ski slope before you know exactly what you're getting into. So, while your fearlessness deserves applause, you might want to slow down a bit and ask yourself exactly what you're risking, and more important, why? Is your thrill seeking propelling you toward a brighter future, or is it just giving you a temporary escape from what you perceive as a humdrum existence?

Step 8. Quash Your Inner Critic

While we have been judged about everything from what we wear to who we call our friends, from our supposed obligations to our sexuality, we have played right into the game by being judgmental ourselves. It is crucial that you break the judgment habit if you truly want to live a free and fulfilled life.

Perhaps you were led to believe that self-criticism facilitates growth. That is absolutely false! The truth is that criticism, whether we are dishing it out or taking it, shrivels our spirit. It makes us feel ugly, and only reinforces the belief that we'll never be good enough. The best place to begin erasing this self-defeating behavior is with yourself. When you can recognize and be proud of the woman you are, you will never feel the need to project negativity because your heart will be full of love—for yourself and for every other human on earth.

Make a list of five things you criticize yourself about—I have provided a sample, but it may not apply to you. Remember, there are no right or wrong answers, just raw feelings.

1. I am fat.
2. _____
3. _____
4. _____
5. _____

Now analyze your list. How long have you been criticizing yourself about the same things? Has your own inner critic produced any positive results? Exactly! Criticism doesn't work—it only makes you feel bad. So be willing to put a halt to it! In order for a child to grow and blossom, she needs love, acceptance, and praise. Replace the five statements above with five loving and supportive alternatives.

1. I am a beautiful person inside and out. I am not defined by my weight.
2. _____

3. _____
4. _____
5. _____

Now let's turn the tables. Face it, we are all guilty of judging other women, even when they are our friends, and even if we justify it by saying we're only teasing. Cattiness is not part of a woman's nature, contrary to popular belief. The need to criticize stems from insecurity and a lack of respect, both for yourself and for the object of your derision. Ladies, we need one another, and when we treat one another badly, we are only playing into the systematic repression of women in general. Who are you guilty of belittling? List five people (they could be friends, public figures, or family members) and write a sentence about the reason for your criticism. Examples: "Michelle. She is so bossy." "Cathy. She dresses like a slut."

1. _____
2. _____
3. _____
4. _____
5. _____

As you did for yourself, take each entry and replace it with a positive remark. There is something that you can admire in each and every woman. Look for qualities (or potential qualities) that celebrate the essence of that woman, that help define who she is in a celebratory way. Examples: "Michelle. She sure has a lot of confidence about her opinions." "Cathy. She must work hard at the gym to carry off a dress like that!"

1. _____

2. _____

3. _____

4. _____

5. _____

From now on, every time you think of the people on your list, praise them rather than tear them down. Keep your mind filled with positive thoughts and make a habit of allowing only positive comments to leave your lips. If you want to stop being judged, then you cannot assume the right to judge others. As you release the compulsion to pick on yourself, you will notice that you no longer feel compelled to criticize others. When you make it okay to be yourself, then you automatically allow others to be themselves. As you stop judging others, they will release the need to judge you. Then everyone enjoys the freedom to be who they are!

 Step 9. Determine Your Sexual Shame Index

How can we claim ownership over our lives when we can't even acknowledge our own bodies and their natural needs and desires? Your physical body is as important as any other aspect of yourself, and it's also the most easily accessible. Why, then, do so many of us have trouble simply looking at ourselves nude in the mirror? Most of our beliefs about sex and sexuality can be traced back to childhood and rules attributed to God and religion.

When we were babies, we knew how perfect our bodies were, and we felt free to touch and examine ourselves without any shame, until we were told otherwise. No girl under a certain age measures her breasts to find her self-worth!

Not surprisingly, men rarely suffer the same low self-esteem issues when it comes to their bodies and their sexuality. I believe this is proof enough that we've been misguided, lied to, and manipulated, because men recognize what we don't: a woman's sexuality equals power over the strongest of men. Along with the capacity to bear children, we were given the ability to experience pleasure. This is another one of those birthrights we must claim ownership of. The exercises below will help you to abolish shame and celebrate your femininity.

Answer the following questions as honestly as you can.

1. What did you learn about sex as a child?

_____

2. What did your parents teach you about your body? Was it beautiful, or something to be ashamed of?

_____

3. What did your teachers or church say about sex? Was it a sin to be punished?

_____

4. What did you call your genitalia? Were they just something "down there"?

_____

5. Do you think your parents had a fulfilling sex life?

_____

6. How are your ideas about sex similar to those of your parents?

_____

7. How are they different?

_____

8. Do you equate sex with love?

_____

9. Were you ever sexually abused?

_____

10. If you could change one thing about sex in your life, what would that be?

_____

Look back at your answers and try to detect any similarities between how your parents approached the topic of sex and how you feel about sex and your body today. If there are similarities, you need to ask yourself if you deserve to form your own opinions or if you are going to continue living by abstract rules that were *not* created with your well-being in mind.

Step 10. Abolish Shame and Celebrate Your Sexuality

Affirmations are positive statements meant to empower us. They help to counteract the negative messages we've been led to believe in, like "Sex is dirty." Changing a negative message into a positive one, like "Sex is beautiful when shared with someone you love," shifts our consciousness. This is an exercise that you can practice as often as you'd like. It's my belief that if you can devote ten minutes to vacuuming, watching TV, or talking on the phone, you can find a little bit of time for yourself and your quest for empowerment . . . every day.

Find a quiet place where you can be alone for at least ten minutes. Sit or lie down, whichever is more comfortable for you, and close your eyes. Try to concentrate solely on your breathing. When you feel peaceful, try to recall all of the messages you have received over the years regarding your body and sexuality. Certain messages will naturally have the most impact. Think carefully: Who is giving (or gave) you this message? What are they saying? How are they behaving? Are these messages verbal or nonverbal?

When you feel ready, open your eyes and write down a single sentence describing the negative message. Then, for every negative message you remember, write down a positive message that offers a new, positive outlook you will adopt for yourself. When you make your statements, always use the present tense: "I am" and "I want," for instance. It's important to live in the now. Here are some examples that might spark your thought process:

- *Negative message:* Women who have sexual feelings are shameful.

   Affirmation: Women are sexual beings and have the right to sexual thoughts and feelings.

- *Negative message:* You must have sex with your husband anytime he wants, no matter what.

   Affirmation: I don't have to do anything I don't feel comfortable doing. The decision to have sex is a joint decision.

- *Negative message:* God doesn't want me to be sexual.

   Affirmation: God created and approves of my sexuality.

- *Negative message:* My partner won't like my body.

Affirmation: My partner reflects the love I have for my body.

- *Negative message:* I am not good enough.
  Affirmation: I love myself and my sexuality.
- *Negative message:* Sex is painful.
  Affirmation: I am gentle with my body and so is my partner.
- *Negative message:* I am afraid of sex.
  Affirmation: It is safe to explore my sexuality.

Step 11. Rewrite Your Belief System

Below is an example of a "Belief Diagram." Ten negative beliefs that can cause you to give your power away are included, along with replacement beliefs that will help you to take your power back. In the blank section that follows on page 213, use your life story for examples of negative beliefs that have affected you personally; then replace them with new, empowering beliefs.

Old Negative Belief	New Positive Belief
I am afraid I will be rejected and abandoned.	No one can reject me unless I give them the power (and reject myself). As I learn to love myself, I regain my power.
I fear the world.	As I face my fears, I embrace the world, understanding that I can handle all that life brings me. With this belief I regain my power.

Old Negative Belief	New Positive Belief
I am afraid of expressing what I need.	Unless I communicate, others don't know me and can't respond. As I accept my own needs and communicate them, the right people will accept me. With this belief I regain my power.
I am afraid of asserting myself.	I accept and express my own truth. It is only when I live in truth that I am free. By living in truth, I regain my power.
Others need to change for me to be happy.	I can choose people who are good for me. When I try to change people, I give my power away. As I choose the right people in my life, I regain my power.
I feel vulnerable.	As I claim myself, and my right to be who I am, I will take my power back.
I am weak.	I can, and will, create what I want for my life, because I trust myself. As I trust myself I regain my power.
I am afraid to look at my pain.	Pain shows me where I need to change in order to realize myself and my potential. As I look at my pain, I regain my power.
I am not good enough.	My identity and worth are my birthrights. I won't blame myself for being human. As I stop judging myself, I regain my power.
It is painful not to be loved, or not to let myself be free to be who I really am.	As I accept, respect, and love myself, others will also. Self-denial equals pain. Self-acceptance helps me to regain my power.

Now create your own diagram of old beliefs and new beliefs.

Old Negative Belief	New Positive Belief

Coming up with a new belief system for yourself won't happen overnight. It may take years, in fact. But with attention and practice, you can make fundamental changes in your life right away. As when you're strengthening your muscles or learning a skill, you must put forth effort. If you catch yourself blindly agreeing with something or someone, take a moment to analyze why. First, you have to investigate the roots of what you believe, then you must develop your own original opinions and values. Finally, you need to commit these new, informed beliefs to memory, so that they can replace the old, damaging ones.

Step 12. Implement Your Newfound Beliefs

Create a *strategic empowerment plan* detailing how you will take back control of your life. Now that you have replaced old damaging beliefs with your new empowering beliefs, you are in a perfect position to determine what goals *you* want to reach. Some goals are easier to wrap your head around than others. Some goals require a more flexible timeline, are dependent on other things falling into place, or perhaps aren't as high on your "must do" list. You should, however, be able to list and analyze at least five major life goals right now.

Have you always wanted to continue your education and become a doctor or an actress or a teacher (or anything *you* dream of)? Do you fantasize about traveling the world? Is your dream to get married and have children? The possibilities are endless, and as you move through the process of self-realization, you'll find that your dreams only grow in number and scope.

Write down three things you have always dreamed of, whether you told anyone or not.

1. _____

2. _____

3. _____

It is essential to commit this plan to writing, and to keep it where you can see it every day. Progress takes determination and we all need reminders. How you organize your strategic empowerment plan is a personal choice. Create your plan to best meet your needs. You might include the specific steps you'll take to reach your goal, a timeline for how long the process should take, what obstacles you may run into and how you can overcome them, the benefits you'll reap by reaching your goal, and how you will continue to grow once you've achieved your goal.

Like many of these exercises, your strategic empowerment plan should be ongoing. Continue to add goals as they occur to you, and realize that you are always allowed to change your mind. If you find that things aren't going exactly as planned, tap into your courage, do whatever it takes, and above all, trust your inner power.

Step 13. Write Your Own "Bill of Rights"

You can think of your own set of boundaries (which will help you live your life as you choose) as your personal Bill of Rights. I wrote my own several years ago and I share them with you below. In the space that follows, create one for yourself—a Bill of Rights that honors everything about you and that will not be compromised under any circumstances.

People will constantly try to push their opinions on other people, swearing that their way is the "right" way, and that your way is "wrong." My stock answer is, "Your way works for you; that's great. My way works for me, and I like it like that."

Yasmin's Bill of Rights

I, Yasmin, have the unalienable right to . . .

1. appreciate my strengths, embrace my weaknesses, and never be ashamed of either.
2. decide for myself what I want and do not want; what I like and dislike; what interests me and what doesn't—and I can be fine with all my opinions, regardless of what anyone else thinks.
3. be my own person, never having to sacrifice my true self for the sake of others.
4. listen to other people's ideas and perspectives while preserving my individuality.
5. disallow anyone from intruding upon my life.
6. have my own views, values, and priorities.
7. protect my emotional well-being from anyone, including family.

Your Bill of Rights

I, _____, have the unalienable right to . . .

_____

_____

_____

_____

_____

_____

_____

Acknowledgments

My journey in life has brought me across wonderful people and beautiful souls. I would like to acknowledge those who have loved me, guided me, supported me, inspired me, sustained me, protected me, healed me, and nurtured me while I wrote this book. I honor you with my deepest love and gratitude.

First, Johanna Castillo, senior editor of Atria Books. Thank you for your faith in who I am and what I do.

Judith M. Curr, executive vice president, publisher, Atria Books. Your vision has made this book possible. Thank you for believing in me and giving me the opportunity to share my message through this book.

My literary agent, Jennifer Cayea, for all your support and dedication to my career.

My editors, Dolores Prida and Patricia Hernandez, whose talents and wisdom have turned my manuscript into a beautiful book.

My HOPE sisters, the University of Southern California's MAAA, Raul Vargas, Dolores and Veronica.

My dear friends Edgar Veytia, Yvonne Lucas, Carrie Lopez, Daniel Gutierrez, Michelle Dulong, Ruth Livier, Nancy Landa, Sylvia Martinez, and Xitlatl Herrera for your enduring love and support.

And my family: my mother, who took care of my daughter day and night until I finished the manuscript; my sisters, who nurtured and guided me; my daughter, Divina, who lovingly waited outside my door when I would write for hours; my niece, Isabella, whose presence makes my day; and my brother-in-law, Michael, for loving all so much.

About the Author

YASMIN DAVIDDS, international bestselling author and empowerment specialist, dedicates her life to the empowerment of women. Yasmin uses the "whole persona" philosophy in teaching people of all ages and backgrounds how to live empowering lives. Many women, particularly Latinas, have changed their futures by learning to take personal responsibility for their lives and finding happiness through self-esteem. She is recognized and continuously highlighted as one of the Top Leading Latinas by *Hispanic Magazine* (June 2003, 2004, 2005) and also as one of the most influential Latinas in *The Book of Latina Women: 150 Vidas of Passion, Strength and Success* by acclaimed author Silvia Mendoza. Through her inspirational speeches, Yasmin delivers a simple but profound message: "People will only treat you the way you allow yourself to be treated. If you want others to respect you, begin by respecting yourself first. That means standing up for yourself and not allowing anyone to mistreat you in any way."

She is the host of the television talk show *The Latina Perspective* and the radio program *¡Adelante mujer!* The groundbreaking *Empowering Latinas: Breaking Boundaries, Freeing Lives,* Yasmin's internationally bestselling book, which is used in university curricula across the country, along with her most recent self-help system, *The Latinas 7 Principles,* are dedicated to women's empowerment, as are her tremendously popular keynote presentations. In Yasmin's eyes, Latinas all over the world have unique, untapped talents, which have gone unrecognized for too long. Her mission is to teach them to embrace their worth and their talent so that they can improve their quality of life.

Since 1989, Yasmin has counseled tens of thousands of men and women, from junior high school to corporate level, acting as an adviser and mentor. Yasmin serves on the board of directors for HOPE (Hispanas Organized for Political Equality) and is a graduate of the HOPE Latina Leadership Institute. She also served as an influential member of the San Diego State University Associated Council, the SDSU Finance Board, and the SDSU Associated Executive Committee. As a member of the board of directors of the USC Mexican-American Alumni Association, Yasmin has been instrumental in providing Latino students with over $1 million in scholarships. In her role as a director for Los Angeles's leading radio station Power 106's Knowledge Is Power Foundation, Yasmin identifies pertinent issues affecting the Latino community and develops programming to address what matters most.

Beyond her experiences as the daughter of Latino immigrants, raised in a predominantly Hispanic neighborhood east of Los Angeles, Yasmin has done extensive research on Latino culture and the Latina psyche, with an emphasis on how cultural messages, including issues such as machismo and self-esteem, affect Latinas. Having worked personally with thousands of Latinas on subjects ranging from drugs and violence to self-respect and goal setting, Yasmin has been gathering material for her unique and powerful personal growth programs for many years. Recently, Yasmin has been devoting her time to her speaking tours, visiting universities, corporations, and a variety of organizations.

Her next book, *You Go, Girl! Raising Powerful Females*, will be published in fall 2006. She is a resident of Los Angeles, where she is the single mother of her six-year-old daughter, Divina.